Multiple Assessments
for
Multiple Intelligences
Third Edition

James Bellanca

Carolyn Chapman

Elizabeth Swartz

SkyLight
Professional
Development

Arlington Heights, Illinois

Multiple Assessments for Multiple Intelligences (Third Edition)

Published by SkyLight Professional Development
2626 S. Clearbrook Dr., Arlington Heights, IL 60005
Phone 800-348-4474, 847-290-6600
Fax 847-290-6609
info@skylightedu.com
http://www.skylightedu.com

Creative Director: Robin Fogarty
Editors: Carolyn Hogan, Julia E. Noblitt, Heidi Ray, Sue Schumer
Formatter: Donna Ramirez
Book Designer: Bruce Leckie
Cover Designer and Illustrator: David Stockman
Production Supervisor: Bob Crump

LCCCN 97-75330
ISBN 1-57517-076-0

1212-McN
Item number 2095

Z Y X W V U T S R Q P O N M L K
06 05 04 03 02   15 14 13 12 11 10 9 8

Contents

Introduction

Howard Gardner's landmark study of multiple intelligences has opened many avenues for improving the process of learning and challenges teachers to explore new instructional practices no matter what the context of their schools. In her book, *If the Shoe Fits…: How to Develop Multiple Intelligences in the Classroom* (1993), Carolyn Chapman provided hundreds of tools, techniques, structures, and strategies for facilitating the development of multiple intelligences in the classroom. Carolyn built on Gardner's assumption, "To my mind, a human intellectual competence must entail a set of skills of problem solving—enabling the individual *to resolve genuine problems or difficulties* that he or she encounters and, when appropriate, to create an effective product—and must also entail the potential for *finding or creating problems*—thereby laying the groundwork for acquisition of new knowledge" (Gardner, 1983, p. 60). Carolyn invited teachers to fit each student with the "best shoes" for exploring the experience of learning. She incorporated the spirit of Gardner's theory by selecting only those rich, varied, and practical instructional tools that usefully translate the theory into sound practice.

Most teachers who wish to integrate multiple intelligences theory into the classroom face a challenge that Carolyn did not address fully in her previous book—*assessment.* Because federal and state education agencies and the general public are calling for schools to be more accountable, assessing student performance is of great concern. Many school districts gear instruction toward standardized tests. Teachers are consequently pressured to tailor instruction to fit the tests. Though this practice contradicts what is known about the best teaching, learning, and assessment methods, the system speaks and the teachers must respond. In this environment, even the most committed teacher finds it difficult to use multiple intelligences-based instruction and the many alternative assessment practices that align with it.

"In our district," quoted the testing director of an affluent Long Island town, "we do *not* teach to the test." However, parents in the district discuss how teachers, pressured by administrators, subtly adjust the curriculum in the weeks preceding the state tests. Sample tests appear "just to familiarize students." Math tasks take on a repetitive character, "because we want the children to do well, and we know the types of questions that will be asked."

In an affluent Chicago suburb, test preparation went to extremes. Parents who noticed major score discrepancies among schools in the same district pushed for an investigation. The board found that a principal purposefully pressured teachers to get students ready for tests. Teachers were advised to match the curriculum to the predicted test questions, to encourage certain students to stay home during test week, and to coach others who were sure to do very well.

These extreme examples may be isolated. On the other hand, many conversations among teachers focus on what they are asked to do to prepare their students for tests. For example, teachers are prodded to spend more time with practice tests from workbooks, to increase the number of pages covered, and to ensure that students work in a quasi-test environment. In this atmosphere, it is no wonder that one teacher protests, "I know what MI will do for my students, but there just isn't time." Another says, "Why multiple intelligences and assessments? There isn't time. We have the district tests."

This book counters such thought. It is designed to align assessment with instructional practices that promote the development of the multiple intelligences. Recognizing that all teachers will not be able to restructure their schools to accommodate Gardner's theory, the authors focus on **aligning the best assessment practices with multiple intelligences theory and practice within the constraints of the existing classsroom.** To highlight emerging assessment alternatives, such as logs and journals, teacher observation check lists, video samples, and portfolios, the authors have elected to imbed assessment of the multiple intelligences in the development of classroom standards and rubrics that set criteria for excellence in student performances. The authors intend not only to fit sound instructional practices within the multiple intelligences framework, but also to ensure that the methods used are appropriate tools for improving what and how students' learning is assessed.

The ideas outlined in this book require change in instructional and assessment practices. How far any teacher can go in effecting such change depends on the individual and the school system. Barriers to change include lack of time and effort. It takes time to learn new ways of organizing instruction and assessment and the effort to switch the curriculum norm from "How many pages did we cover?" to "How well do the students understand the concepts and develop their potential?" The barriers are very evident when changing to alternative and authentic assessment. Observation check lists, interviews, double-entry journals, and teacher-made tests take more time to assess than Scantron tests of basic skills.

To facilitate use of multiple assessments for the multiple intelligences, the information in this book is designed to be transferable to the classroom. Chapters one and two place assessment standards in a context beneficial to all teachers and students. Chapters four through eleven center on assessment of a specific intelligence, though the majority of classroom learning framed by Gardner's theory does not focus on a single intelligence. Even in classrooms that are mandated to instruction in a single discipline, such as geometry or American history, or in a single lesson, such as mastery of science vocabulary for a grade-level test, using multiple intelligences theory permits the teaching of several different intelligences simultaneously. Thus, in a math lesson, the teacher may use cooperative groups (interpersonal), hands-on manipulatives (bodily/kinesthetic), and logs (intrapersonal) as tools to accomplish the logical/mathematical task.

The demand for the teacher to focus on a single subject does not prevent him or her from using authentic assessment devices. Nor does it prevent use of multiple intelligences strategies. The teacher can use his or her own assessments to measure content mastery. In addition, he or she can use an observational check list based on a precision standard to note how accurately each student solves the problems and completes the calculations. Finally, the teacher can review the students' logs to gain greater insight into each student's understanding of the problem-solving processes used. If necessary, the teacher can even grade each of the assessments against a standard and mark the grade book accordingly.

While each chapter gives specific ideas for assessing a specific intelligence, the possibilities are endless. To the degree that a teacher applies multiple intelligences practices, the students will receive a more comprehensive picture of what they know and do, a more insightful picture of what they can do in the future, and better tools to take responsibility for their own learning. Teachers benefit by having multiple ways to teach each child and multiple ways to assess what works and doesn't work.

To assist you in using the ideas and methods in this book, the authors' team used the three-story intellect model that Robin Fogarty and Jim Bellanca developed in *Patterns for Thinking, Patterns for Transfer* (1993). The model, suggested by Julie Casteel, a staff developer in Waterford, Michigan, is based on a quotation from Oliver Wendell Holmes.

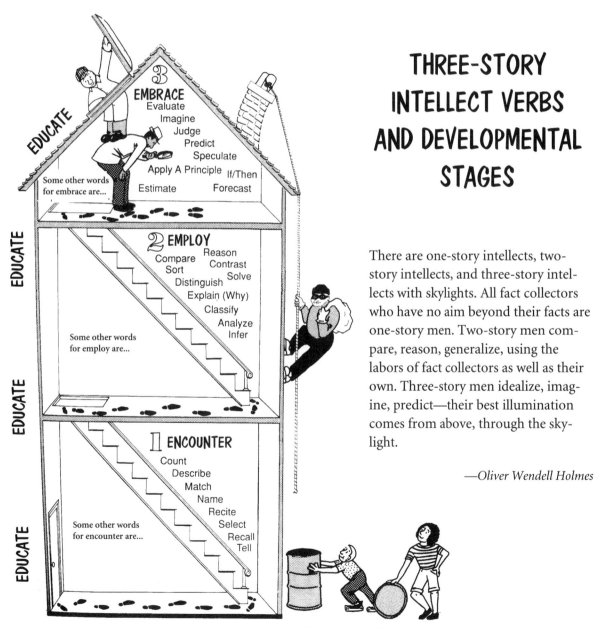

THREE-STORY INTELLECT VERBS AND DEVELOPMENTAL STAGES

There are one-story intellects, two-story intellects, and three-story intellects with skylights. All fact collectors who have no aim beyond their facts are one-story men. Two-story men compare, reason, generalize, using the labors of fact collectors as well as their own. Three-story men idealize, imagine, predict—their best illumination comes from above, through the skylight.

—*Oliver Wendell Holmes*

(Adapted from Bellanca & Fogarty, 1991. Used with permission.)

The authors begin chapters four through eleven with operational definitions of the multiple intelligences. They then expand the definition with commentary and examples that promote a clearer understanding of Gardner's intent. They also develop an understanding of how to arrive at classroom performance standards for each intelligence. Finally, the authors provide guidance for constructing the performance standards and assessment tools that are most useful for the development of the targeted intelligence.

One of the greatest challenges for a teacher is individualizing instruction. Similarly, one of the great challenges for the authors is to write a book that allows readers to customize the information. The authors of this book have found the three-story intellect model valuable in meeting the challenge. At the first level, the authors provide the information that gives all readers a common reference point. This foundation helps the reader construct useful rubrics and effectively evaluate the students in his or her classroom. At the second level, the authors facilitate individual understanding of how each intelligence fits by developing performance standards and alternative assessment tools. Through commentary and examples, the authors clarify how the concepts and strategies fit in the classroom. Finally, at the third level, the authors give structured closure tasks designed for application.

Ultimately, this approach provides the flexibility needed to make assessment easy at any grade level. Whether an individual teaches in a traditional grade school with rows, chairs, workbooks, and report cards; a special education class, including behaviorally disordered youngsters pulled from the mainstream; an untracked chemistry class with behaviorally and/or physically challenged students included with mainstream students; or a school of the future based entirely on Gardner's multiple intelligences theory, there is opportunity to make practical use of the concepts and strategies suggested.

Every classroom has restraints on what modifications a teacher can make without official "permission." Each district and state varies in curricular flexibility. Many teachers work in school districts where state- and/or district-mandated tests drive curriculum and instruction toward lower-level outcomes. These outcomes promote the memorization of isolated facts and bits of information. In some cases, especially in the sciences, compulsory tests force teachers to teach outdated and erroneous information. In other cases, as in math and writing, the tested outcomes promote low expectations and minimal performance. Requirements for mastery of such isolated skills as "recognizing a gerund," "distinguishing an umlaut," or "adding two-digit fractions," channel the teacher toward repetitive practice of these isolated, lower-level skills. At the same time, the teacher is channeled away from helping students apply the foundational skills to write a coherent letter or essay, comprehend the meaning of a well-written story, or solve mathematical problems.

Other teachers work in school districts where covering the curriculum is tightly controlled. The justification for tight control is usually the specter of a standardized test. In New York, high school teachers feel pressured to teach to the Regents. In Michigan, the Michigan Assessment of Educational Progress is the target.

From the national SAT and ACT tests to state-standardized tests, myths and unsubstantiated stories abound on what each test "covers." The tests become the scapegoat for regimented coverage of the curriculum. In other cases, test content is neither myth nor mystery. Overt and continuous pressure is put on teachers to do exactly what the state test was designed to do—hold teachers accountable for covering basic skills.

To promote the quality of their schools to parents and communities, administrators and school boards may use a variety of devices to keep teachers accountable. Out-of-control accountability takes the focus away from learning. Some use an accountability focus on test results. This focus controls what and how much material is covered each day. In the worst possible scenario, all teachers at all grade levels teach the same page in the same textbook or workbook at the same time. In other scenarios, the principal monitors daily lesson plans, samples weekly student work, and visits classrooms to enforce standardized coverage. In still other high-control scenarios, high school departments post unit test scores on preestablished dates for comparison of results. Elementary principals identify the topics most likely to be tested, schedule the time allotted to cover the topics, and evaluate teachers on their ability to stay "on task, on time."

At first glance, such rigid standardization may appear unnecessary. The unannounced rationale for standardization is making the curriculum teacher-proof. A teacher-proof curriculum should prevent mavericks from electing to do their own thing and omitting elements of the curriculum they deem unimportant.

A closer look reveals the shortcomings of such a mechanistic approach. First, it makes individualized instruction impossible. Second, it causes metacognitive benefits to be lost. Third, it reduces curriculum to textbook and workbook coverage and the testing of low-order outcomes. Fourth, it ignores all the research on the importance of mediated learning and socially constructed meaning. While the focus on accountability may satisfy a few, research says that it does not improve teaching and learning. On the contrary, research correlates the lowest test scores with teachers who obscure real learning by following the textbook-coverage curriculum.

Rigid standardization may be possible and even necessary on an assembly line. For instance, a carmaker sets precise quality standards. As each car comes off the assembly line, an inspector examines the car to establish how well it measures up to the standards. If the acceptable standard for defects is .017, the car with .018 does not meet that standard. A total quality company determines how many items fail to meet the standard, looks for the cause, and eliminates the problem in the production process. Rigid application of the quality standard is possible even to a six sigma (99.999999 correct/.000001 mistake), as practiced so successfully by Motorola.

Schools lack the capability to standardize in the same way and to the same degree as engineers and scientists. Few companies are close to the standard of six sigma. However, many educational psychometricians exaggerate the potential of their educational measurements and highlight the similarities of their work to the work of their peers in the hard sciences. Anyone comparing a physicist's or engineer's data measurements with an educational psychometrician's data measurements can readily see how the scientist's hard data suppresses in sophistication and application the yet emerging tools of the educators.

Those who work objectively with educational measurement recognize that tools capable of measuring six sigma in teaching and learning are a distant and questionable ideal. Precise measurements are limited not only because the available educational measurement tools are so primitive, but also because the process of human learning is so complicated.

Standardized tests, other than having some predicting value, do little else than please opportunistic politicians and school administrators whose student populations are geared to do well. Seldom are these tests used to examine the system-imposed learning process in search of its defects. Often they are used to punish a teacher or principal for not having a class or school "up to standard" or to force teachers into more rigid adherence to a weak standard.

The first error in applying educational standards occurs when the perfect test score is made the goal. In a quality-controlled industry, a six sigma VCR may be a perfect VCR. However, the VCR comprises many other standards that have to be met in a variety of different ways. A single measurement of a single component does not merit the six sigma rating. It is one variable. The six sigma standard is not intended for making a judgment about a single VCR. The goal is not to label the best VCR nor to rank-order all the rest. The goal is to determine the mean number of defects and to identify which can be eliminated by improving the production process. When the assessor of finished products reviews the many different variables and totals the defects, the computer program pinpoints causes, tallies totals, and makes it possible to change how the VCRs are made.

A second common error in applying educational standards is treating the student as a product (as in "the products of our school"). Students are not inanimate objects that are easily stamped "approved" or "rejected." Even before Gardner identified multiple intelligences, we knew that students were far too complex for quick stamps of approval, letter grades, or numbers as a measure of their capabilities (Kirschenbaum et al., 1971).

Someday, when educators gain a better understanding of human growth and brain functions and when they have more effective measurement tools, we may obtain better insights into how human beings really learn. Until that time, however, our best hope is to develop accurate, valid, and reliable assessments and focus them on improving the teaching process and helping all students take greater command of, and responsibility for, how they learn.

In the meantime, school districts should help teachers develop new assessment tools, new understanding of standards, and better ways to use these tools and standards to improve teaching and learning in their classrooms. Rather than trying to duplicate the standards possible in the sciences, teachers need to develop more fluid, adaptable performance standards which measure student performance and improve the learning process for all students. Likewise, teachers need time to develop reliable measurements that help them identify and correct the defects in the teaching-learning process so that all students come closer to the high performance standard. Such an approach is usable with any student in any classroom without the need for rationalizations involving heritage, race, challenged condition, age, sex, curricular approach, or instructional method. This approach can enhance learning in the most traditional classroom. Integrating multiple intelligences theory across all disciplines will transform learning from a lower-level recall event to a higher-level challenge for all students. In addition, when traditional testing, grading, and reporting are demanded in a school district, the teacher who uses better assessment tools has more comprehensive data to report to each student's parents, and more students will take home improved test scores and grades.

To facilitate the development of multiple assessments, study all the material in this book as if you had no constraints on using the ideas. Imagine that a respected financial backer has invited you to test-fly seven hot-air balloons. You will have complete charge of how far and how high you go in the trials. You are not allowed to merely look at them and study the working parts—you must fly each one. Each of the balloons is somewhat similar, and you have no idea of exactly what will happen in each flight. You just have to know yourself well enough to determine how far you can go in each trial.

Working with such an attitude helps you expand your possibility thinking. This is the pattern of thinking that Edward de Bono (1985) puts under the "green hat." As you wear this hat, it is more likely that you will be more open in exploring the new assessment approaches that might work best. You will also be less likely to make a premature or shortsighted judgment. After you have gathered all the possibilities for your ideal assessment of an intelligence, you will quickly find out whether you are ready to facilitate more learning by all your students.

If you are a solo user of this text, you can make your reading interactive in several ways. First, take notes on your computer, in the columns, or in a notebook. Second, highlight ideas that strike you as useful, different, or enlightening. Third, debate with the text in column notes. Fourth, use the note summary section at the end of each chapter to summarize the key elements. Finally, complete your own model applications at the end of each chapter, try them in your classroom, and assess their effectiveness.

Use this text with colleagues and you may find at least one who is interested in authentic assessment. After each of you studies a chapter solo, get together to discuss (a) the information gathered, (b) what sense or nonsense the information makes, and (c) the possibilities for trying out your favorite ideas in your classrooms. Use the key verbs for each level of the three-story intellect (page vii) to construct your discussion questions (e.g., first story—"What are the key terms we need to define in this chapter?"; second story—"How are these ideas similar to and different from what we are already doing?"; third story— "How can we use these ideas in future lessons?").

After each of you has tried out the ideas, bring your observations, student artifacts, and other data to discuss (1) what worked well, (2) what you want to change, and (3) what advice or feedback you want from colleagues. Weigh your results and move to the next chapter for a collaborative study.

We recommend that you keep the artifacts, notes, and responses in a folder that will become your portfolio. At the end of your study of the text, review all the application data you produced, throw out what you found least helpful, and refine what you retained.

If you have the opportunity, find a colleague who is already practicing some of these ideas and invite him or her to share experiences and mediate your group's discussion. As a discussion mediator, he or she can ask key questions that assist each of you to clarify your understanding and discoveries about performance assessments in the classroom. The best discussion mediators will cause you to think about what you plan to do, what you have done, and how you can refine your applications.

Please note that it is not the intent of this book to explain the multiple intelligences theory or its implementation in the classroom. Rather, this book explains *assessment* through multiple intelligences. Readers who are new to the idea of multiple intelligences can learn about the theory and practice in *If the Shoe Fits...: How to Develop Multiple Intelligences in the Classroom* (IRI/SkyLight Publishing, 1994) by Carolyn Chapman; *Multiple Intelligences: A Collection* (IRI/SkyLight Publishing, 1995), edited by Robin Fogarty and James Bellanca; and *Frames of Mind: The Theory of Multiple Intelligences* (Basic Books, 1983) by Howard Gardner. By understanding the theory and practice, you will have a clearer, stronger grasp of what is explained in this book.

The Assessment Challenge: Assessing Classroom Standards

Understanding standards means starting with some assumptions about what the word *standard* means. For the ancient Greeks, the standard was the banner or flag that marked each military legion in an army. In addition to the nation-state's colors, the standard usually was embossed with a symbol that represented the virtues the nation-state valued. Thus, the Spartan army's standard bore the Minotaur; the Athenian standard carried the golden sun, the symbol of Apollo, the god of wisdom. All who fought under the banner were expected to exemplify the characteristics represented by the standard.

A more modern definition of standard captures the tone of the industrial age. A *standard* is an established rule used to measure quantity and quality. The standard is considered to be a reliable and authoritative norm that indicates what is best. For instance, in the most literal sense, there is a standard weight for every coin produced by the U.S. Treasury. There is a standard set by the FAA for the proper mix of cement, sand, and water in an airport runway used by jumbo jets. Such standards are fixed by study and usually do not change.

Content, lifelong, and performance standards

In education, there are other definitions. Some argue that a standard in education is any task that requires the use of important knowledge and skill in specific content areas. These are often called *content* standards. Others use the term *standard* to describe knowledge and skills that transcend content areas and subject disciplines and have application for life. These are called *lifelong standards*. Finally, there are those who would define an education standard as a norm, established by reliable and authoritative practitioners, against which academic performances are measured in order to determine the quality and quantity of a student's ability to apply knowledge and skills to new and fresh situations. This is called a *performance* standard.

The performance standard integrates both the content and the learning process standard, and requires that all learning be for transfer at higher cognitive levels. This is the definition that is used in this book. Artificial distinctions between content and process are not needed. Neither is it necessary to think that only some students can attain a standard. In the performance standard, different criteria describe to what degree a student attains a standard.

When applying standards to the measurement of quality of student learning, it is important to be wary of too literal a match between the industrial use of a standard and the educational use. Measurable criteria make it relatively easy for a manufacturer to control the quality process. In some cases, quality is assessed by mechanical testing equipment: an audiometer to measure noise volume; a computerized emissions control unit to measure exhaust emissions; and a scale to record weight. In other cases, inspectors and line workers are trained to look for visible signs or indicators.

Student learning, however, is more difficult to assess. Since the turn of the century, many educators have tried to make the school resemble a factory and students resemble a product. Many practices, including much of the testing done for so-called accountability purposes, are attempts to make schools operate as assembly lines producing look-alike, act-alike graduates who meet a measurable product standard. Because industry can control the quality of its raw materials, its assembly process, and its equipment with measuring devices at times more sophisticated than the product itself, it can construct very controllable standards, criteria, and quality indicators. And, as most psychometricians and educators acknowledge, education cannot come close to replicating industry's control over its raw materials and measurement tools.

Exit standards

For learners to take control of, and responsibility for, their own learning, external manipulation must give way to internal motivation. It is in this shift that the quality process has its primary value in the classroom. It becomes the teacher's responsibility to facilitate and mediate the shift. In practical terms, the process begins with the school's identifying exit standards.

The school community aligns its exit standards with its vision of excellence for graduates and any state-mandated standards. Three to five exit standards are more than enough to guide student performance through the years that the student is enrolled. In each elementary grade or secondary course of study, teachers select one to three school exit standards. They align their classroom standards to the exit standards to guide the assessment of all projects, lessons, and study units. As students mature in this system of standards, teachers gradually increase student involvement in designing the rubrics with their criteria and indicators of success. (A rubric is a rule or guideline that outlines the criteria and indicators of success. The indicators are observable measurable behaviors which show to what degree the student is using knowledge and skill. The criteria are the benchmarks which tell to what degree the student is attaining the standard.) The aim is that each student would be able to set up and assess his or her own rubrics and that each candidate for graduation would conduct a self-directed study based on a rubric for excellence that he or she constructed.

In the classroom or school built on the theory of multiple intelligences, a middle grade faculty might select exit standards aligned with development of the multiple intelligences. In the design of its exit rubrics, the faculty might elect the standards of accuracy, problem solving, collaboration, creativity, and metacognition. In language arts, teachers could elect to target the verbal/ linguistic intelligence and use the interpersonal, intrapersonal, visual/spatial, and musical/ rhythmic intelligences as support. Consider the following example.

MIDDLE GRADE EXAMPLE

The faculty targets what it wants all students to do with the writing process before sixth grade graduation.

Topic: Process Writing

Targeted Intelligence: Verbal/Linguistic

Supporting Intelligences: Interpersonal, Intrapersonal, Visual/Spatial, Musical/Rhythmic

Targeted Standard: Metacognition — The student plans, monitors, and assesses how well he or she completed an assignment that required him or her to write an original essay or story based on school experiences this year.

The faculty designs its rubric.

▪ THE RUBRIC ▪

Targeted Standard: Assessing the quality of one's own writing process (Metacognition)

Tool: Assessment Essay

CRITERIA

High Performance: After completing the writing assignment, the student adds a four- to five-page written evaluation detailing how well he or she planned, monitored, and assessed the quality of work done.

    Indicators: No spelling or grammar errors
                     All complete sentences
                     Beginning paragraph, three to seven middle paragraphs, and closing paragraph
                     Two or three examples per middle paragraph
                     Clear transitions
                     Notes pluses and minuses
                     Experiences chosen show originality
                     Firm grasp of writing process

Sound Performance: After completing the writing assignment, the student adds a three- to four-page written evaluation detailing how well he or she planned, monitored, and assessed the quality of work done.

    Indicators: Occasional spelling or grammar errors
                     Mostly complete sentences
                     Beginning paragraph, three to five middle paragraphs, and closing paragraph
                     One or two examples per middle paragraph
                     Notes some pluses and minuses
                     Grasps most important elements of writing process

(Continued)

Adequate Performance: After completing the writing assignment, the student adds a one- to two-page written evaluation detailing how well he or she planned, monitored, and assessed the work done.

Indicators: Occasional spelling and grammar errors
Jumbled sentence structure with more than three incomplete sentences
Beginning, middle, and ending paragraphs
One or two examples per middle paragraph
Notes only pluses
Fuzzy on elements of the writing process

Not Yet: After completing the writing assignment, the student adds a one- to two-page written evaluation detailing how well he or she planned, monitored, and assessed the work done.

Indicators: Numerous spelling and grammar errors
Lack of sentence structure
No clear beginning, middle, or ending
Unable to identify pluses or minuses
Little understanding of the writing process

This rubric requires the following multiple intelligences instruction during the sixth grade as content develops the verbal/linguistic intelligence and process develops the intrapersonal and logical/mathematical intelligences.

Verbal/Linguistic:
        Spelling
        Grammar
        Sentence structure
        Paragraphing
        Use of examples
        Transitions
        Essay or story organization
        Writing process

Intrapersonal:
        Personal experience
        Weighing pluses and minuses of experience
        Self-evaluation of writing ability

Logical/Mathematical:
>   Organization of essay
>   Logical connection of examples
>   Connection of ideas with transitions

The rubric also implies how sixth grade teachers can best prepare students for the metacognition standard. They will need to provide instruction and assessment tools that enable students to have:

- Facility in analyzing a personal experience
- Facility in evaluating through the use of pluses and minuses
- Knowing the ingredients or parts of the writing process
- Evaluating own performance in use of the writing process
- Knowing the importance of planning a writing task, monitoring the task, and assessing the task when done
- Being aware of planning, monitoring, and assessing the task in progress

With the exit rubric planned, the teacher teams can attend to assessment rubrics for guiding more specific skill development.

Note, in the *standard,* the emphasis in the three-story model is at the second level that "explains how" each student developed an essay plan or outline. The content is embodied in knowing (first level) and in using (third level) a process for planning an essay. This presupposes that the students knows the elements of a well-written essay, can write such an essay, and can explain how he or she wrote the essay. These "ingredients" target the verbal/linguistic intelligence, while the associated or supportive intrapersonal intelligence calls for a reflection on the writing process.

In a traditional format, the rubric might have this appearance:

Targeted Intelligence: Verbal/Linguistic   **Tool:** Matrix

Supporting Intelligences: Intrapersonal, Logical/Mathematical

THE RUBRIC

Targeted Standard: Metacognition — Each student explains how he or she planned his or her essay on _____.

CRITERIA

High Performance: After writing the essay, the student tells the class how he or she included a beginning, a middle, and closing paragraph without cuing.

(Continued)

Indicators: Identifies the paragraphs in order; labels without assistance
Explains content of paragraphs
Gives reasons for structure

Sound Performance: After writing the essay, the student tells the class how he or she included a beginning, a middle, and closing paragraph with some cuing.

Indicators: Identifies the paragraphs in order
Labels with some assistance
Explains content of some paragraphs

Adequate Performance: After writing the essay, the student uses the bulletin board outline to explain how he or she used a beginning, middle, and closing paragraph.

Indicators: Identifies the paragraphs
Matches paragraphs with bulletin board outline
Explains main idea of essay

Not Yet: After writing the essay and using the bulletin board, the student requires additional cuing in order to explain the paragraphing used.

Indicators: Cannot label paragraphs
Requires assistance to match paragraphs with outline
Cannot explain main idea of essay

In the more usable format, the rubric would take the appearance of the sample on the following page. In this rubric, which is in matrix style, note that individual criteria are indicated in the left-hand column of the rubric. Each column shows a different level of performance, with the numbers shown in the column headings representing indicators of success or performance level—"1" being low and "4" being high. To rate a student, determine his or her numerical score for each of the four criteria, then add up the four scores to determine the total. If the evaluation is in the context of summative assessment, the final score may be converted to a grade via a scale—at the teacher's discretion.

THE RUBRIC: PLANNING AN ESSAY

Standard: Plans and writes a three-paragraph essay.

Criteria	1	2	3	4
Identifies Needed Paragraphs	unsure of what is needed	identifies paragraphs one-two with cues	identifies all paragraphs with no explanation	identifies paragraphs and explains beginning, middle, and end
Labels Each Paragraph	mislabels all	labels one to two correctly with cues	labels two correctly— no cues needed	labels three correctly—no cues needed
Explains Transitions	weak rationale	explains one transition paragraph with cues	identifies two transition paragraphs	identifies and explains all transitions
Explains Content	vague explanations	requires cues to explain	explains two paragraphs correctly	explains three paragraphs correctly

Comments:

_____

_____

_____

Final Grade: _____

Scale	
_____	= A
_____	= B
_____	= C
Below ___	= Not Yet

Exit rubrics require the most preparation. When a teacher team collaborates within the multiple intelligences framework and targets specific standards, the task is much easier. For instance, language arts teachers write their verbal/linguistic rubric for metacognition, while the math team prepares a logical/mathematical rubric for metacognition (e.g., the student solves a pre-algebra math problem and writes an essay detailing how he or she planned, monitored, and assessed the problem-solving process).

The social studies team might select a different standard, such as collaboration. Their rubric could focus on the interpersonal intelligence, demonstrating a cooperative problem-solving task in social studies (e.g., invent the best form of government for operating this class without a teacher) that shows how students work together using cooperative skills mastered during the year (e.g., using first names, taking turns, doing one's job, and encouraging others). The rubric outlines the expected performances that the teacher measures with a check list of cooperative behaviors and that the students write about in a journal entry. In addition, the rubric lists indicators that helped in the assessment of the student's knowledge of the forms of government studied and his or her ability to transfer that knowledge to a life situation (the class). Finally, the description of the task and the rubric would guide students to use the visual/spatial intelligence by asking each student to make a diagram of the decision-making process that the new government would use.

For the final exit assessment, the other teachers who work with the sixth grade team (e.g., P.E., special education, fine arts, science) can develop their own targeted exit rubrics or collaborate in an integrated rubric among themselves or with the other teams. The more collaboration and integration of rubrics within the team, the easier the creative task will be and the more creative and challenging the exit assessments will be.

Guidelines for creating rubrics

Once exit assessments are completed, the task of producing project and unit assessments can fall in place. These guidelines help ease the task of creating the first rubrics and help students take full advantage of them.

Follow the KISS principle

Keep rubrics short and simple. Assessment is not instruction, but should align with instruction to help students keep a focus. One exit rubric per year is sufficient for primary children. In the middle grades, two or three are enough. In secondary school, one well-developed rubric per course aligned with five or six exit standards is preferable to a host of superficial rubrics.

Post and review exit rubrics in all classrooms

As the year progresses, relate each project or task to the exit standards. For instance, when teaching a specific problem-solving process, discuss with students how the specific project will help them with the exit rubric before starting the instruction. Just as it is helpful for all in the family to know their destination before leaving on a trip, it is helpful for students to know the destination of a lesson.

Post and review major project and lesson rubrics

Connect these to the exit rubrics. Have students identify how the specific rubric is similar to and different from the exit rubric.

Involve students in framing lesson and project rubrics

After several lessons in which you provide rubrics, have students brainstorm possible indicators for a lesson rubric. Next ask students to help frame criteria. "How will you know you are doing a good job?" Discuss this question and use cooperative groups to frame the task criteria. Finally, discuss the standards. What do the words mean? How would those standards look outside class? Assign students to interview parents, local community business people, artists, and officials about these standards in their adult lives.

Communicate the exit rubrics to parents

At the beginning of the year, send a letter that discusses your standards and how you will use them to help students become more responsible. Explain the variety of assessment tools you will use and how your use of multiple intelligences benefits the child. At the first parent conference, show the parents how the rubric works. Detail how you use it to promote development of the multiple intelligences. Also review each student's strongest intelligence and show his or her performance on a rubric. Finally, have available samples of work that correspond to the criteria and indicators in a rubric.

Watch your verbs

Just as verb choice is critical in the three-story intellect (page vii), verb choice is also critical in constructing rubrics. If you choose your verbs from the top story, you will accomplish two important objectives. First, you will communicate that the application of learning to other areas is what your classroom is about. Your application rubric will drive your students to the most complex thinking. As they individualize their own learning applications, they will find themselves enjoying the responsibility of controlling their own learning. Second, the choice of a third-story verb allows you to construct three-story lessons and projects more easily. To get to the third story, the students will have to work more diligently to gather and process information before they work on the projects.

Highlight the big picture

Save yourself the time and trouble of constructing a rubric for each minute skill in your curriculum. Don't confuse standards-based assessment with outcomes-based education or mastery learning.

If you follow the KISS principle, you will find a most valuable use of your time is in the preparation of the exit rubrics. If you find yourself in long committee meetings devoted to developing rubrics for every minute skill and concept (as do many school teams involved in writing course outcomes), you will know that assessment has gotten out of proportion.

Maintain an academic focus

Today's overloaded curriculum demands selective abandonment of what is taught each day. The primary purpose of school is academic learning. The well-selected classroom curriculum focuses learning on the core content that will best prepare students to live and work in the coming decades. By using multiple intelligences theory as your filter, you can select those academic disciplines that align well with Gardner's eight intelligences and fit students' needs to understand academic concepts they will use after they leave your classroom. Thus, the disciplines of math, language arts, science, the fine arts, and physical education may continue as the academic content most important in the classroom. Within each discipline, however, the theory of multiple intelligences enables you to discard outdated content so you will have time to develop students' critical understanding and enhance development of their multiple intelligences.

Writing a complete multiple intelligences rubric is not difficult. Nor should it be time consuming. The following examples provide models for you to use in writing your classroom rubric. Note the highlighted (boldface) items that need your attention.

As with the exit rubric that aligns with each intelligence, the teacher can identify which intelligences are used to support the targeted intelligence. Use the sample rubric on page 3 to construct a lesson rubric useful to your students' development of the intelligence you select.

Sample Rubric: Verbal/Linguistic

TARGETED INTELLIGENCE: Verbal/Linguistic

SUPPORTING INTELLIGENCES: Visual/Spatial, Intrapersonal

THE RUBRIC

Standard: Completes an essay analyzing Walter Lord's novel *A Night to Remember.*

Criteria	1	2	3	4
Five-Paragraph Structure	no start or end	starting paragraph only	starting and ending strong	middle paragraphs also strong
Theme Identified	theme announced	one point carried through all paragraphs	two points made	middle paragraphs each develop a point in the theme
Clear Transitions	no transitions	one to two transitions	three transitions	appropriate transitions between each section
Examples from Text of Novel	no examples	incorrect examples cited	one correct example in each middle paragraph	two to three examples in each middle paragraph

Comments:

_____

_____

_____

Final Grade: _____

Scale	
_____ = A	
_____ = B	
_____ = C	
Below ___ = Not Yet	

SECONDARY

Sample Rubric: Verbal/Linguistic Lesson

TARGETED INTELLIGENCE: Naturalist
SUPPORTING INTELLIGENCES: Verbal/Linguistic

THE RUBRIC: RESEARCH PROJECT

Standard: Expresses ideas clearly in essay.

Criteria	1	2	3	4
Clear Intention or Purpose in Beginning Paragraph	no apparent purpose in opening paragraph	purpose is implied but not clear	thesis statement clear	strong thesis statement; supporting sentences are clear statements of purpose
Middle Paragraphs Capture Steps in Research Process	most process or steps in research missing	missing two or three key steps	missing a step or has fewer than two examples per step	middle paragraphs relate with several examples each to thesis
Content Is Valid and Accurate	content is shallow and shows no insight	content is accurate but lacks insight	content is accurate with some questions left unanswered	content of research is 100% accurate and meets standards of validity
Closing Paragraph Is an Accurate Summary	no tie to theme and/or subtopics	vague theme or subtopic connection	closing ties to theme and subtopics	closing paragraph ties to theme and captures all subpoints with a punch!
Grammar and Syntax Appropriate	multiple mistakes	four or more errors	two to three errors	no errors in spelling, syntax, and grammar

Tools: Score sheet based on four indicators

Comments:

_____

_____

_____

Final Grade: _____

Scale	
_____	= A
_____	= B
_____	= C
Below ___	= Not Yet

Make Your Own

LESSON TITLE:

GRADE OR COURSE:

TARGETED INTELLIGENCE:

SUPPORTING INTELLIGENCES:

THE RUBRIC

Standard:

Criteria	1	2	3	4

Comments:

_____

_____

_____

Final Grade: _____

Scale

_____ = A

_____ = B

_____ = C

Below ___ = Not Yet

Multiple Strategies for Multiple Assessments

In the traditional classroom, the teacher has very few tools for evaluating a student's work. In the elementary grades, he or she can grade computations, examine vocabulary and reading workbooks, and check standardized tests by counting correct answers. The teacher can also grade writing samples and teacher-made essay tests by counting mistakes in grammar, spelling, and punctuation and by giving points for good ideas.

In the secondary classroom where lectures dominate, quizzes and multiple-choice tests are the favored evaluation options. For the most part, grading is simple and straightforward. How many blanks have correct answers? How many answers are true or false? How many times did the student make the correct choice of four? If teachers are lucky, the school has a Scantron machine that will help them escape the tedium of marking the what, when, where, and who questions. Of course, after each test or quiz, the teacher is still left with entering another set of grades in the grade book and computing an end-of-year total.

In the multiple intelligences classroom, the possibilities for assessing student learning are as numerous as the options for organizing what and how students learn. Although assessment drives instruction in the traditional classroom, assessment and instruction are partners in the multiple intelligences classroom. This is possible, as Carolyn Chapman demonstrated with more than 300 authentic learning strategies in *If the Shoe Fits...: How to Develop Multiple Intelligences in the Classroom* (Chapman, 1993), because the process approach of multiple intelligences instruction calls for active and authentic learning that engages all students in the construction of their learning.

Where does authentic assessment start in the multiple intelligences classroom?

The authentic assessment of learning in the multiple intelligences classroom begins with more authentic learning. Authentic learning is that which replicates as closely as possible situations that students will encounter outside school. Instead of sitting at desks filling in work sheets or having their heads filled with facts they will reproduce on more work sheets, multiple intelligences students are up and running. Sometimes working alone, sometimes with other students, and sometimes with high technology, these students work in the classroom as if they were in an office, store, or laboratory. The teacher organizes the day, structures the task, and gives help as needed. To enrich the learning and to ensure that each child is challenged to develop all the intelligences, the teacher mediates the tasks so that the students understand what they are learning.

There are many options for structuring authentic, active learning opportunities to develop each intelligence.

Exhibits

Students research a topic and prepare an exhibit to display what they have learned. In past generations, exhibits at science fairs, 4-H fairs, and art shows were limited to the "best students," as the school or club attempted to win competitions and bring home trophies and ribbons. Exhibits were also prepared for extra credit or required extracurricular work. In the multiple intelligences classroom, however, construction of exhibits is a learning experience open to all.

PRIMARY EXAMPLES

Students study the food groups and make a poster display
Students study Egypt and make a display of famous architecture
Students read *Ann of Green Gables* and create a bulletin board of her life
Students visit the zoo and make an ad campaign to save the animals

MIDDLE GRADE EXAMPLES

Students research the water quality and make poster board displays
Students set up an art gallery of their work for the year
Students build models of space stations and show the stations with the architectural designs
Students study authors and make collages to represent the authors' ideas

SECONDARY EXAMPLES

Driver's Education students prepare an exhibit on the dangers of drinking and driving
English students create concept maps of dramas read and hang them in a hall display
Architecture students build model houses for display on parents' night
Computer students show middle graders how graphic displays are made
Science students make a science fair with projects for parents' night

---

Performances

Students participate in a show of multiple talents for their peers, parents, other classrooms, or audiences such as senior citizens and school neighbors. In the past, performances were limited to special classes, such as music, drama, or extracurricular, seasonal events. In the multiple intelligences classroom, performances may include all children in the classroom preparing a musical production or a pageant for their families and friends, or the performance may engage a single child preparing to read a poem or short story to the class.

PRIMARY EXAMPLES

Each cooperative group picks one story to read and enact for the class
The class studies the pilgrims and invites other classes to see a live diorama
The class enacts life in the pioneer days for parents and teachers
The class performs winter songs for the school
A child reads his or her summer adventure story to the class

MIDDLE GRADE EXAMPLES

Groups pick an event from American history and role-play for the class
Groups create rap songs about characters from a novel
A student reads his or her poem to the class
The class prepares a documentary video about the environment to show to the board of education
Groups write cigarette, alcohol, and drug abuse playlets to present at a school assembly

SECONDARY EXAMPLES

English students write dramas for the school radio station
Physics students show elementary students "the magic of science"
Dance students create original works for the local community theater presentation
American history students create skits for the different periods of history
A student plays a self-made folk instrument to his or her American history class

---

Journals and logs

The journal or log is a personal learning history. It enables students to make connections, examine complex ideas, and think about novel applications of the curriculum over a period of time. The journal is not limited to language arts or English class. It is a tool all students can use to develop their communication skills in all the intelligences and in all subject areas.

PRIMARY EXAMPLES

Students use stems to start ideas.

Today I learned. . . .

I am glad that. . . .

A friend is like_____because. . . .

Students make webs with pictures.

Students evaluate their work with happy face scale.

MIDDLE GRADE EXAMPLES

Students use stems to start assessments.

I do my best work when. . . .

My strongest intelligence is. . . .

I can improve_____by. . . .

Students construct KWL for each new book.

Students use right angle, Venn, and matrix organizers as reading strategies.

Students sketch representations of science experiments.

SECONDARY EXAMPLES

Algebra students record problem-solving strategies.

Chemistry students sketch chemical reactions.

English students use stems to analyze characters in stories.

_____is like a (animal) because. . . .

The character most important to this story was_____because. . . .

World history students use Venn diagrams to compare cultures.

Demonstrations

A student shows others how to do a process. This is especially helpful for learning mathematics, science, fine arts, and health topics. Demonstrations challenge students to take factual material (ordinarily left to memorization) and turn it into a presentation that they must organize and explain. In preparing to teach, the students delve more deeply into the topic. Audiences for the demonstrations may be other classes, teachers, parents, peers, or community members.

PRIMARY EXAMPLES

Students show younger children how to write a story.

Student pairs show animal care.

Students explain how to make patterns with pattern blocks.

MIDDLE GRADE EXAMPLES

Students show how to do CPR to the class.

Students demonstrate science safety rules.

Students demonstrate how characters in a story could have solved the story problem in a different way.

Students show how to build a model plane, car, or house.

Students show how to stretch for warm-up.

SECONDARY EXAMPLES

Science students show how to do an experiment.

Math students show how to do a math problem.

History students show how to make an artifact from a specific culture.

Art students show how to throw a pot from a culture studied in world civilization.

Products

Students make objects that are the end result or product outcome connected to a learning unit. Often, products are replicas of art works or multimedia presentations of key concepts. Products are especially helpful in challenging students to make cross-disciplinary connections when studying in a particular discipline such as history or science. Products are the result of a "learn-by-doing" approach. They are especially effective when combined with journals and exhibits.

PRIMARY EXAMPLES

Students write and draw story books.

Pairs make soap sculptures of famous buildings.

Cooperative groups make community dioramas.

Cooperative groups make government collages.

MIDDLE GRADE EXAMPLES

Students make model charts of the problem-solving process.

Teams make a video story.

Students write essays and stories about famous scientists.

Pairs make mobiles on characters in a novel.

Groups design costumes for colonial history pageant.

Cooperative base group creates team flags.

SECONDARY EXAMPLES

Math students design geometric buildings.

Biology students make models of human anatomy.

Physics students build model bridges to test stress.

English students create a class concept map of literature they have read and write a five-page report.

Graphic art students design computer logos.

Problem-solving process

Students apply problem-solving techniques in a variety of curricula. Historically, curriculum in American schools is organized by scope and sequence of factual materials and basic skills. The multiple intelligences classroom—based on Gardner's theory that the human intelligence must encompass problem-solving capacity as well as the ability to create problems and, therefore, learn (Gardner, 1983)—works at its best when problem solving is the core of the curriculum. In this context, the curriculum emphasizes a process, not information. Students learn how to apply the problem-solving process as the key learning tool. No matter what the curriculum content or the intelligences targeted, students apply their developing problem-solving skills.

This approach is significantly different from the traditional organization of curriculum and instruction in two ways. First, problem solving is the starting point. It is not something that classes merely "get to" when they show mastery of the basic skills or have covered the textbook. Second, problem solving is the basic tool for all students. In the past, many districts have saved problem solving for the gifted children. In the multiple intelligences classroom, all students *start* with learning how to problem solve across the curriculum.

PRIMARY EXAMPLES

Pairs use colored blocks to form patterns and analyze the process.
Students brainstorm endings to a story.
Groups of three weigh bricks to estimate total number of bricks.
The class brainstorms solutions for walking home safely.
Base groups meet once a day to discuss how they are solving problems in the
      lunchroom, playground, cooperative groups, etc.

MIDDLE GRADE EXAMPLES

Pairs solve two-step word problems in math with think-aloud strategies.
Student teams interview senior citizens to explore solutions to community problems.
Student groups role-play historic figures solving historic problems.
Students write mystery stories for other students to solve.

SECONDARY EXAMPLES

Sociology students solve sample social problems faced by contemporary individuals.
English students use problem solving as a theme for studying literature.
Chemistry students use community pollution problems as a way to apply chemistry theory.
U.S. history students change history by changing decisions about the atomic bomb.

Graphic organizers

Students use visual formats to gather, analyze, and evaluate information. To encourage students to take a "learning-how-to-learn" approach to standard text material, teachers use cooperative groups to teach students the graphic information organizers appropriate to each of the intelligences. Independent follow-up assignments enable students to demonstrate individual command of the learning organizer.

PRIMARY EXAMPLES

The class creates a web about the good qualities of the school and selects the three best.
Teams fill a Venn diagram comparing two continents.
Students make concept maps of their neighborhoods.
The class creates a T-chart on cooperation.
Students use sequence charts to plot the steps in a story.

MIDDLE GRADE EXAMPLES

Pairs use Venns to compare characters in a short story.

Cooperative groups use targets to evaluate local politicians.

The class creates a concept map of the science curriculum.

Students diagram sentences by famous authors.

SECONDARY EXAMPLES

English students create concept maps in their journals for characters in novels.

World civilization teams use Venns to contrast major historic figures.

Biology students use matrices to analyze animal classifications.

Earth science lab groups use right angle organizers to transfer environmental principles to their community.

Projects

Students construct and create meaningful long-term projects that incorporate several intelligences. In secondary English classes, the junior research paper on American literature is a familiar project. In junior high school, planning the graduation trip to Washington, D.C., or the state capital is a popular project. In the multiple intelligences classroom, project-centered learning appears across many disciplines. At the beginning of the year, cooperative teams learn how to organize a project and, by the end of the year, students are engaged in a variety of individual and group projects.

PRIMARY EXAMPLES

Students communicate through Internet with students in other states and countries.

Students visit a senior citizens home where stories are shared.

Students collect samples of leaves for making posters.

Students study a major health problem and make a pamphlet.

MIDDLE GRADE EXAMPLES

Students design and build go-carts to test acceleration.

Student teams write short stories for a class book that they will exchange over Internet with classes in other countries.

Students create challenging math problems to send over Internet to other classes.

Students plan, write, and produce a video about the literature they are reading.

SECONDARY EXAMPLES

Industrial arts students design, build, and sell a house.

Student groups make music videos with classical music.

Biology students start a community animal shelter with a local veterinarian.

English students interview senior citizens for a special edition of the school newspaper.

Civics students investigate interpretations of a controversial law by different generations.

Art students clean graffiti from the rail station walls and paint a historic mural.

Interdisciplinary study students plan a trip to England and raise the funds by making a video on British art, history, and literature with the local public television station.

WHAT IS INTELLIGENCE?
(a working definition)

The ability to solve problems of consequence in a particular cultural setting.

Gardner (1983, p. 63)

Multiple Tools for Multiple Assessments

What tools are available for assessing these authentic learning tasks?

The multitude of learning strategies available to stimulate the multiple intelligences creates numerous opportunities for assessing student learning. Once the teacher has selected the ways students will address topics in the curriculum, he or she can select one of many tools for assessment. When judiciously selected, these instruments can provide more information about what and how the student learns than is possible using only standardized tests. This matrix highlights some of the possibilities. When deciding on which tools to use with a strategy, check the matrix with your choices.

Tools \ Strategies	Exhibits	Performances	Journals & Logs	Demonstrations	Products	Problem-Solving Process	Graphic Organizers	Projects
Double-Entry Responses								
Observation Check Lists								
Observation Note Cards								
Likert Scales								
PMI Charts								
Open-Ended and Guided Responses								
Teacher-Made Tests and Quizzes								
Graphic Organizers and Designs								

Double-entry responses

This tool promotes a two-way conversation between student and teacher. It works especially well in the journal. As students work through a project, the teacher asks the students to write comments on the work they are doing and to submit samples of that work. Using the rubric as a guide, the teacher comments on the indicators as they relate to the student's work. He or she gives suggestions from the rubric on how the student can improve the quality of his or her performance. The student responds to the suggestions, and the dialogue continues to the end of the project.

JOURNAL

Student Entry

Today, I finished the design of the costume for the Duchess of York. I found the design at the museum store. Since I am shorter than the duchess was, I had to do lots of adjusting in the pattern. I have included the original design and my changes. I worked to make the changes very precise. 12/14

I redid the sleeve measurements. It's a good thing. I would have had extra long arms. My receipts and addition are enclosed. I'm getting ready to cut the fabric. This will take lots of care on my part. To be authentic, my costume has lots of fancy ruffles on the cuffs and the neck. My mom says that I will be the most precise tailor in the world if I pull this off. 1/3

Teacher Comment

I am pleased with how you found your design. You also did a good job in adjusting the design to fit your size. I checked your calculations. You need to recalculate the sleeve length. 12/27

Your math is now 100% exact. You are doing "wow" work in the three indicators you have worked on. 1/5

EXAMPLE RUBRIC

Class: _Sophomore English_   Project: _Shakespearean Costumes_
Student: _Lisa Franconi_
Team: _Mary Smith, Kate Bell, Lisa Franconi, Quinn Heart_
Standard: _Precision_
Task: _Each student designs and makes a costume from Shakespearean times. They enact a playlet that shows the four people at dinner after the play_ Romeo and Juliet.

THE RUBRIC

Indicator 1:   The costume is an authentic reproduction in every detail.

Wow   O.K.   Not Yet

5---3---0

Indicator 2:   The costume is crafted with precise attention to sewing, color match, etc.

Wow   O.K.   Not Yet

5---3---0

Indicator 3:   The playlet shows how the characters would most likely act after the play. Specific references are made to the play.

Wow   O.K.   Not Yet

5---3---0

Indicator 4:   Students keep daily journals detailing the steps of their work.

Wow   O.K.   Not Yet

5---3---0

Indicator 5:   Each keeps a precise record of the expenses for the project.

Wow   O.K.   Not Yet

5---3---0

Grade: A/21   B/17   C/12   D/7

In the space on the next page, fill in a dialogue you might have with a student concerning the rubric. Make a new rubric or use one already created for your class.

Make Your Own

CLASS: _____   **PROJECT:** _____

STUDENT: _____

TEAM: _____

STANDARD: _____

TASK: _____

┄┄┄ THE RUBRIC ┄┄┄

Indicator 1:

Wow   O.K.   Not Yet

5--3--0

Indicator 2:

Wow   O.K.   Not Yet

5--3--0

Indicator 3:

Wow   O.K.   Not Yet

5--3--0

Indicator 4:

Wow   O.K.   Not Yet

5--3--0

Indicator 5:

Wow   O.K.   Not Yet

5--3--0

Grade: A/21   B/17   C/12   D/7

Observation check lists

The teacher creates a check list based on the rubric. He or she can use these check lists at specific intervals as students are working or create check lists for student observers to use. It is better if check lists vary among the intelligences. After the check lists are done, the teacher may use them for a class discussion and/or put them in portfolios. According to Gardner's theory, check lists need to focus more on the process of learning than on the final product. This communicates to students the importance of the process of learning.

PRIMARY EXAMPLE

SOCIAL SKILLS CHECK LIST
ASSESSMENT OF TEAMWORK SKILLS

Dates: 10/21
Class: 3rd Grade
Teacher: Forbes

Ratings:
+ - Frequently
✓ - Sometimes
○ - Not Yet

Who	Listening — Skill 1	Using First Names — Skill 2	Taking Turns — Skill 3	Encouraging — Skill 4	Sharing — Skill 5	Celebrations
1. Lois	✓	✓	○	✓	✓	Dropped in 2 areas
2. Connie	**+**	**+**	○	✓	**+**	
3. James	✓	✓	✓	✓	✓	
4. Juan	**+**	**+**	✓	**+**	**+**	Improved in 2 areas
5. Beth	○	○	**+**	✓	✓	
6. Michele	✓	✓	○	✓	✓	
7. John	✓	✓	○	✓	✓	
8. Charles	**+**	**+**	○	✓	**+**	
9. Mike	✓	✓	✓	✓	✓	Went from 5 O's to this in 2 months
10. Lana	**+**	**+**	✓	**+**	**+**	

COMMENTS: Work with Lois on a regular basis. Change her seat and group.

Burke (1993, p. 111)

Make Your Own

Directions: Select the skills you want to observe and write them on the five slanted lines at the top.

OBSERVATION CHECK LIST

Dates: _____
Class: _____
Teacher: _____

Ratings:
+ - Frequently
✓ - Sometimes
○ - Not Yet

Who	Skill 1	Skill 2	Skill 3	Skill 4	Skill 5	Celebrations
1.						
2.						
3.						
4.						
5.						
6.						
7.						
8.						
9.						
10.						

COMMENTS:

MIDDLE SCHOOL EXAMPLE

OBSERVATION CHECK LIST

Student: _Denise_   Class: _Science_   Date: _12/5_

Type of Assignment: _Problem-solving skills_

		Signed	
☐ Teacher	Date_____	Signed_____	
☐ Peer	Date_____	Signed_____	
☒ Self	Date_ _12/5_ _	Signed _Denise Smith_____	

	Frequently	Sometimes	Not Yet
PERSISTENCE			
• Checks work	X		
• Revises work		X	
• Stays on task		X	
PROBLEM SOLVING			
• Identifies problem	X		
• Brainstorms	X		
• Evaluates alternatives	X		
SOCIAL SKILLS			
• Does role		X	
• Follows guidelines			X
• Listens		X	
ACCURACY			
• Computation correct		X	
• Follows steps		X	
• Checks answers		X	

COMMENTS _____

_____

_____

Burke (1993, p. 111)

Make Your Own

OBSERVATION CHECK LIST

Student: _____   Class: _____   Date: _____
Type of Assignment: _____

☐   Teacher   Date_____   Signed_____
☐   Peer   Date_____   Signed_____
☐   Self   Date_____   Signed_____

	Frequently	Sometimes	Not Yet
_____			
• _____	____	____	____
• _____	____	____	____
• _____	____	____	____
_____			
• _____	____	____	____
• _____	____	____	____
• _____	____	____	____
_____			
• _____	____	____	____
• _____	____	____	____
• _____	____	____	____
_____			
• _____	____	____	____
• _____	____	____	____
• _____	____	____	____

COMMENTS _____
_____
_____
_____

SECONDARY SCHOOL EXAMPLE

PROJECT CHECK LIST
ASSESSMENT OF PROJECT SKILLS

Dates: <u>10/21</u>
Class: <u>10th Grade</u>
Teacher: <u>F. Swartz</u>

Ratings:
+ - Frequently
✓ - Sometimes
○ - Not Yet

Who	Action Plan — Skill 1	Design — Skill 2	Teamwork — Skill 3	Creativity — Skill 4	Standards — Skill 5	Celebrations
1. Toni	✓	+	○	○	✓	
2. Casey	+	+	○	✓	+	
3. James	✓	✓	○	✓	✓	
4. Juan	+	+	✓	+	+	
5. Beth	✓	✓	✓	✓	✓	
6. Michele	✓	✓	○	✓	✓	
7. Judy	+	○	✓	+	+	
8. Charles	○	○	+	✓	✓	
9. Dave	✓	+	○	✓	+	
10. Lisa	+	+	✓	+	+	

COMMENTS: _____

Burke (1993, p. 111)

Make Your Own

Directions: Select the skills you want to observe and write them on the five slanted lines at the top.

OBSERVATION CHECK LIST

Dates: _____
Class: _____
Teacher: _____

Ratings:
+ - Frequently
✓ - Sometimes
○ - Not Yet

Who	Skill 1	Skill 2	Skill 3	Skill 4	Skill 5	Celebrations
1.						
2.						
3.						
4.						
5.						
6.						
7.						
8.						
9.						
10.						

COMMENTS:

Observation note cards

The teacher carries a packet of index cards or adhesive notes with his or her grade book. He or she identifies five to seven students per day to observe at work. As the targeted students work, he or she observes them alone and in a group one to three times that day for a specific intelligence. For each observation, the teacher describes what the student is doing. He or she may use a rating scale such as "doing great," "moving along," and "not yet," or if grades are required, a number scale. To save time, some teachers use a duplicating machine to make standardized cards with a space for the date, the student's name, and the selected intelligence. This helps the teacher focus on observing one intelligence at a time. After the observation, the student reads the card and puts it into his or her portfolio.

PRIMARY EXAMPLE

NAME: *Tommy O'Brian*   DATE: *May 15*   GRADE: *3*
INTELLIGENCE: *Bodily/Kinesthetic*

Mixed feet during square dance practice

Danced to own rhythm

Reversed hand clasps

Not yet

MIDDLE SCHOOL EXAMPLE

NAME: *P. J. Amas*   DATE: *October 13*   TITLE: *Interpersonal*

\+ *Listened in group*

− *Did job*   *Comments: Sat silent the whole time in group except to say good job; looked out window sometimes*

\+ *Encouraged*

− *Contributed ideas*

SECONDARY EXAMPLE

NAME: *Elizabeth Overton*   DATE: *February 22*   TITLE: *Geometry II*

Made group review the directions
Took notes on process
Listened to each team member
Asked "why" several times
Double-checked calculations on calculator   *Rating 5+*
Did job helping with circles
Encouraged a lot

Make Your Own

NAME:_____ DATE:_____ INTELLIGENCE:_____

_____

_____

_____

_____

_____

RATING: _____

Likert scales

This is the most popular and easy-to-use measurement tool for a rubric. It is also easy for students to use in their self-assessments. Some teachers will go so far as to have students attach two Likert scales to every portfolio entry: one by the teacher and one by the student. Peers in cooperative groups may also do scales for their groups or for individual members in the groups.

There are a variety of options for the design of the scale. If grades are required, use the number or letter grade options.

Wow	O.K.	Not Yet
Top Dog	In the Middle	Buried in the Pile
Accurate	Some Mistakes	Inaccuracy
Strong Logic	Some Fallacies	No Logic
Shares Large Group	Shares Small Group	Nonverbal in Class
5	3	0
A	C	F

PRIMARY EXAMPLE

VERBAL SKILLS SCALE

Name: *Mary*　　　　　Date: *May 19*

1. ORAL LANGUAGE

1-------------------------------(-3-)-------------------------------5

Nonverbal
in Class

Talks with
Friends

Speaks in
Sentences
in Class

2. READING

1--------------------------------(-3-)--------------------------------5

Reads Own
Name

Knows Key
Words

Sounds Out
Words

3. WRITTEN LANGUAGE

(1-)--------------------------------3--------------------------------5

Scribbles

Can Write
First Name

Can Write
Words

Burke (1993, p. 67)

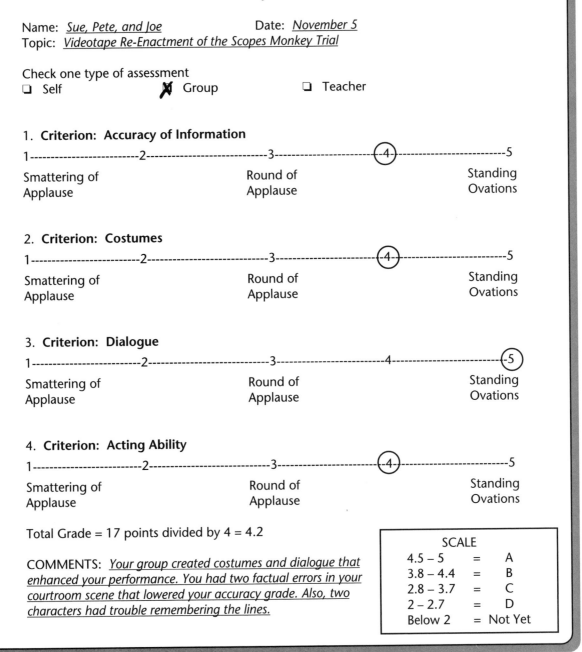

MIDDLE SCHOOL EXAMPLE

VIDEO PROJECT SCALE

Name: _Sue, Pete, and Joe_   Date: _November 5_
Topic: _Videotape Re-Enactment of the Scopes Monkey Trial_

Check one type of assessment
❑ Self   ☒ Group   ❑ Teacher

1. **Criterion: Accuracy of Information**

1---------------------2---------------------3---------------------④---------------------5

Smattering of   Round of   Standing
Applause   Applause   Ovations

2. **Criterion: Costumes**

1---------------------2---------------------3---------------------④---------------------5

Smattering of   Round of   Standing
Applause   Applause   Ovations

3. **Criterion: Dialogue**

1---------------------2---------------------3---------------------4---------------------⑤

Smattering of   Round of   Standing
Applause   Applause   Ovations

4. **Criterion: Acting Ability**

1---------------------2---------------------3---------------------④---------------------5

Smattering of   Round of   Standing
Applause   Applause   Ovations

Total Grade = 17 points divided by 4 = 4.2

COMMENTS: _Your group created costumes and dialogue that enhanced your performance. You had two factual errors in your courtroom scene that lowered your accuracy grade. Also, two characters had trouble remembering the lines._

SCALE		
4.5 – 5	=	A
3.8 – 4.4	=	B
2.8 – 3.7	=	C
2 – 2.7	=	D
Below 2	=	Not Yet

Burke (1993, p. 67)

SECONDARY EXAMPLE

AMERICAN LITERATURE SCALE

Name: _Katherine Burke_   Class: _American Literature_

Instructions to the Student: _Please use this rubric to assess your journal entries for the past six weeks. I will complete a similar form when I collect the journal and apply a point total for your quarterly grade. The journal assessment counts as 20 percent of the quarterly grade._

1. Originality of ideas

3------------------------------2---------------**X**--------------1----------------------------------0
Genius   Creative   Interesting

2. Evidence of synthesis and analysis in thinking

3----------------**X**--------------2----------------------------1----------------------------------0
Genius   O.K.   Not Yet

3. Makes connections

3----------------------------------2--------------------**X**----------1----------------------------------0
Genius   O.K.   Interesting

4. Uses concrete examples

3----------------------------------2-----**X**----------------------1----------------------------------0
Many   Some   None

5. Gives full explanations

3-----**X**---------------------------2----------------------------1----------------------------------0
Many   Some   None

Make Your Own

Name: _____   Class: _____

Project: _____

Instructions to the Student: _____
_____
_____
_____

1. _____

_____   _____   _____

2. _____

_____   _____   _____

3. _____

_____   _____   _____

4. _____

_____   _____   _____

PMI charts

Edward de Bono (1983) invented PMI charts as part of his pioneering thinking skills program. Teachers around the world use this simple and powerful tool to teach students how to evaluate their own learning. Variations include the Like-Dislike T-Chart and the Helpful-Not Helpful T-Chart. When first introducing this method to students, select an all-class learning activity in which the students can brainstorm pluses (P), minuses (M), and interesting questions (I). Next, use it with cooperative group projects and the standard rubric. Finally, when students are familiar with the tool, use it with individual projects and the standard rubric for an intelligence. If grades are required, use a fluency standard and scale the number of acceptable responses (e.g., 12 = A, 10 = B, 8 = C, 6= D) before putting the charts in the portfolio. Use a duplicating machine for multiple copies of a group assessment chart. If possible, duplicate the rubric on the back side so that students can focus their charts on the +, -, ? of the rubric.

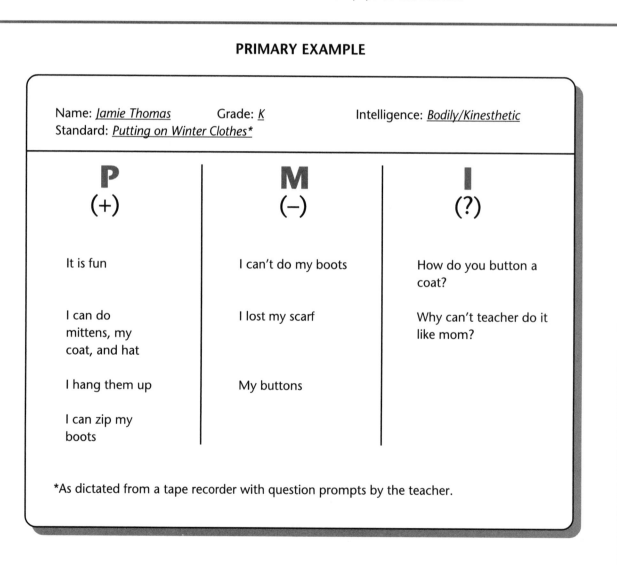

PRIMARY EXAMPLE

Name: _Jamie Thomas_   Grade: _K_   Intelligence: _Bodily/Kinesthetic_
Standard: _Putting on Winter Clothes*_

P (+)	**M** (−)	**I** (?)
It is fun	I can't do my boots	How do you button a coat?
I can do mittens, my coat, and hat	I lost my scarf	Why can't teacher do it like mom?
I hang them up	My buttons	
I can zip my boots		

*As dictated from a tape recorder with question prompts by the teacher.

MIDDLE SCHOOL EXAMPLE

Name: _Mildred Law, Mary Jane Vicks, Fernando Ramirez, Lewis Ali_
Date: _May 5_   Intelligence Target: _Verbal/Linguistic_
Standard: _Cooperative Problem Solving_

P (+)	M (−)	I (?)
All listened	Argued about directions	Why did we have to work in a group?
All reviewed how to problem solve	Took too long	
Helped with first step	Mildred got mad and left	Why does Mildred always get mad?
All gave ideas	It was hard	
Got right answer	We won't get a grade	Why won't we get a grade?
All worked hard	Did we do this right?	

Sample Lesson

"Plus-Minus for Today" Cards

PURPOSE: To enable students to assess each day's learning

ACTIVITY:

When there are less than 10 minutes left in the day, give each student a 3 × 5-inch index card. Ask each student to write a "plus," a positive item about the day's learning experience, on one side of the card and a "negative" item on the other side, labeling the card with "+" and "-" accordingly. (You may want to specify that no names of other students be used in their commentary.) Collect the cards and read random samples to the class.

APPROPRIATE USES:

1. Focus on ideas/topics covered in class for that day only.

2. Do on a regular basis so that students are expecting to be asked.

3. If you must give feedback, simply say "Thank you" or "That is an interesting thought."

VARIATIONS:

1. Postpone the reading of samples until the next day. Start that class with selected statements from the previous day.

2. For middle school and high school, do the card activity once a week.

SECONDARY EXAMPLE

Name: _Tom Ostler_   Subject: _Computer Science_
Topic: _Identifying Crash Cause_   Assessor: _John Smith_

P (+)	**M** (–)	**I** (?)
Found cause of computer failure	Missed the cause of the problem on first diagnosis	Was this preventable?
Saved two computer disks containing data	Worked too fast	Do I need to alter the computer system to prevent this problem?
Replaced a faulty circuit board	Lost one computer disk containing data	Should I create a back-up system in case this happens again?
Applied problem-solving solution		
Kept my cool		

Make Your Own

Name:_____   Subject:_____

Topic:_____   Intelligence:_____

P (+)	**M** (−)	**I** (?)

Open-ended and guided responses

Open-ended and guided responses provide a helpful way to encourage students to think more on their own and not merely parrot what they believe the teacher wants to hear. When these responses are first used, students accustomed to one-word answers, having the teacher do all the evaluating, or answering to only what they think the teacher wants, have a difficult time thinking for themselves. If grades are required, the teacher may have to use the fluidity standard (number of acceptable responses in a chart) and an insight standard (how much understanding does the student show) to motivate start-up of this approach. By modeling with the whole class how to use one of the models, the teacher can "prime the pump" and make students more comfortable with the idea that "what the teacher wants is insightful thinking."

The two most frequently used models of open-ended responses are Mrs. Potter's Questions (Fogarty and Bellanca, 1989, pp. 230–231) and What? So What? Now What? (Fogarty and Bellanca, 1989, p. 235).

Mrs. Potter's Questions

Mrs. Potter's Questions are questions for students on how they learned or how they completed a task. The questions should focus on the *process* of learning, but also work well on the *products* of learning. Providing the rubric for the students to use as a prompt will keep the responses focused on the standards, criteria, and indicators of the process being assessed.

> What did I/we do well?
> If assigned the same task, what would I/we do differently?
> What help do I/we need?

PRIMARY EXAMPLE

All class responds to Mrs. Potter's Questions after a field trip to a museum. The teacher records the answers on the blackboard or an overhead. After reviewing the rubric, the teacher asks the questions and the students respond. To encourage all students to contribute, he or she may call one name at a time or do a simple wraparound with each student taking a turn in order of seating in the classroom.

THE STANDARD: Helping Each Other

THE INDICATORS: Help each other with winter clothes
                  Agree on answers
                  Fill in all answers together
                  Hold hands with partner going to and from bus
                  Hold hands in the museum

Go to bathroom together
Put lunch in same locker at museum
Eat together and clean up together
Wear name tags
Listen to each other
Listen to instructions

What did we do well on the field trip?

Listened to the guide
Listened to the teacher
Listened to the mothers
Held hands all the time
Held hands in the museum

Held hands in the bathroom line
Talked in small voices
Didn't run and scream
Said "thank you"
Sat in our bus seats

What could we do better on the next field trip?

Stay in line
Don't giggle at the guide
Be neat
Have more pencils
Don't get lost
Finish the paper
Don't holler on the bus

What help do we need?

How to find the bathroom
A map of the whole place
To do the answer sheet

MIDDLE GRADE EXAMPLE

NAME: *Susan Stroud*   TEAM: *6A* DATE: *9/29*

EXHIBIT: Science Project/Trip to Mars
INCLUDED PRODUCTS: Ship model, space suit design, ship design, math calculations for fuel use, daily log, three artifacts from Mars
STANDARDS: Problem solving, accuracy, creative thought

What did I do well?

My ship model won first place in the class contest. The judges told me that my design earned top points in accuracy and creativity. My blueprint was loaded with details. I used materials that didn't cost any money. My log was also very thorough. I even recorded the conversations our team had when it did the calculations. The judges also liked the rocks I found on Mars.

What would I do differently?

I wouldn't let the team make me the ship commander. There is too much responsibility in that job. Because I like to write, I would keep my ship's log. I would also be more careful in my calculations. Our team argued about how to figure the fuel load. We didn't have enough to get back alive. That is important. And I would look for some better artifacts than just rocks.

What help do I need?

I need to stop arguing with Jack. He thinks he knows everything. I want to find a better way to show him how to do the math right. I don't know what to say to him when he acts so smart.

SECONDARY EXAMPLE

NAMES: John Stockman, Janet Smith, Adrienne Lindsey, Ian Thomas
PROJECT: Starting a Business/Desktop Publishers, Inc.
INTELLIGENCES: Interpersonal, Logical/Mathematical, Visual/Spatial, Verbal/Linguistic
STANDARDS: Persistence and patience in creative problem solving

What did we do well?
- Used cardstorming method to identify goals and tasks
- Divided responsibilities
- Listened to each other
- Sought consultant assistance
- Noted barriers to success and found answers
- Assessed progress as we went along
- Made a full business plan that was funded

What could we do differently the next time?
- Keep timelines
- Stick to plan
- Listen to consultant advice
- Let Adrienne do the calculations instead of John
- Curb desire to make everything too fancy

What help do we need?
- Faster computers
- More accurate facts and figures

Make Your Own

NAME: _____

COURSE: MULTIPLE ASSESSMENTS _____

DATE: _____

PROJECT: *Applications of This Book's Information Made in the Classroom* _____

INTELLIGENCES: _____

STANDARDS: _____

INDICATORS: _____

_____

What have I applied well?

_____

_____

_____

What can I do differently with future applications?

_____

_____

_____

What help do I need?

_____

_____

_____

What? So what? Now what?

"What? So what? Now what?" is the second open-ended model that promotes assessment. As with Mrs. Potter's questions, these questions are appropriate for student self-assessment or for teacher assessment. The following examples focus on using the model in a double-entry journal. Before use, the teacher must instruct the students in using the model. "What?" refers to "what did you learn?" "So what?" refers to the implications of what was learned. It is a question designed to promote the transfer of learning. "Now what?" asks the students to decide what action will come from their insights. It asks the teacher to suggest actions. As with Mrs. Potter's questions, it is necessary to use this model many times so that students learn to use it well.

PRIMARY EXAMPLE

The teacher uses a tape recorder with groups of three students at the end of a learning center project. She structures the questions and the students take turns giving responses. A note in each student's portfolio tells where the tape is stored.

"What was easy for you to do at this (bodily/kinesthetic) center?"
- Writing numbers in the sand
- Acting out our spelling words
- Using blocks to do math problems
- Dressing up to dance
- Acting parts from stories we read
- Doing sit-ups and counting to 100
- Playing numbers together
- Playing "this is my friend."

"What was hard for you at this center?"
- Dancing the vegetable parts
- Making the human machine work
- Being a machine part
- Being a shape
- Pretending to be a sound

"So how do you think the center helps you learn?"
- I can do the things when I pretend.
- It makes me healthy.
- I like to play games.
- It is fun to move.
- I feel better.

"Now what will you do?"
- I will come back to this center.
- I will be a better friend.
- I can practice my counting and do exercises.
- I can be a TV star.

MIDDLE GRADES EXAMPLE

After a field trip, each student makes journal entries.

What three things did you like most at the museum?
- the coal mine
- the aquarium
- the dinosaurs

So What will you do with what you learned?
- I'm going to build my own aquarium at home. I want a banana fish.

Now What do you intend to do?
- I'm going to save my newspaper route money to buy the materials.

SECONDARY EXAMPLE

Following a unit of study, the teacher can ask each group to list its responses on newsprint.

What were the most important characteristics of the main character?
- outspoken
- brave
- hot tempered
- faithful
- intelligent

So What can you learn from the main character?
- I can learn not to shout out answers.
- I can learn to control my temper.
- I can learn to think through my answers.

Now What will you do with what you learned?
- Let others speak in the group.
- Count to 10 when angry.
- Listen to others' ideas.

Make Your Own

NAMES: _____

PROJECT: _____

INTELLIGENCES: _____

STANDARDS: _____

PRODUCT: _____

"What did we learn?"

_____

_____

_____

_____

_____

"So why is this important?"

_____

_____

_____

_____

"Now what will we do with what we learned?"

_____

_____

_____

_____

Sample Lesson

Guitar Gator

TARGETED INTELLIGENCE: Musical/Rhythmic

SUPPORTING INTELLIGENCES: Interpersonal, Visual/Spatial, Verbal/Linguistic, Logical/Mathematical

THINKING SKILLS: Comparing and contrasting, drawing conclusions

SOCIAL SKILLS: Listening, responsibility

CONTENT FOCUS: Music, brainstorming

MATERIALS: Newsprint and markers, overhead

TASK FOCUS: This is a cooperative task. Use groups of three. Give groups large sheets of newsprint and one to three colored markers.

PRODUCT: An ad

PROBLEM: To identify forced relationships among unlike groups.

ACTIVITY:

1. Present the students with these 5 rules for brainstorming

   B = Build on each others' ideas

   U = Use the far out

   I = Invent, invent, invent many answers

   L = List everything and anything

   D = Do stretch your ideas

   Ask students to explain "the key" message behind the "BUILD" process and to give examples of how it may work in a brainstorming session.

2. Explain how, when we are generating new ideas, our tendency is to stay safe and secure in what we perceive is "the right way" or "the acceptable answer." By forcing ourselves to look at old ideas in new ways, we can discover, invent, and propose new ideas. BUILD gives us the rules or guidelines, even the mindset, to stretch our thinking process. Sometimes a strategy such as "Guitar Gator" is used as a thinking tool to force business professionals to explore new and different "looks" in advertising and public relations. It also helps writers, artists, and film directors give us a new look at something "old." You may want to show your own illustration of an alligator combined with a guitar at this point, or have a volunteer student draw such a creature. To get your students thinking, ask what new animal characters they have seen on television cartoon shows lately.

3. On the chalkboard or using an overhead projector, show a chart such as the following one, making two columns. Column A should be labeled "Musical Instruments." Column B should be labeled "Animals."

4. Following the "BUILD" process, have students brainstorm each list. Complete column A before column B. After column A is full, cover it so that students don't try to match columns. Number each response in each column, as shown.

A. Musical Instruments	B. Animals
1.	1.
2.	2.
3.	3.
4.	4.
5.	5.
6.	6.
7.	7.
8.	8.
9.	9.
10.	10.
11.	11.
12.	12.

5. From a hat or box containing slips of paper numbered from 1 to 12, ask a student to pick 2 numbers. Circle the numbers on the chart, one from each column.

6. Pair up students in random fashion. Give each pair a sheet of newsprint and ask them to sketch a new animal that combines the physical characteristics of both the selected animal and the selected instrument. Have students give names to their creations.

7. Hang all the sketches at the front of the class.

8. Ask student teams to identify their new animal/instrument, describe its characteristics, and tell how it might be useful or valuable. Follow-up with questions such as:
   a. What could be the worst possible effect this _____ has on people?
   b. What would happen if you brought a _____ to your house?
   c. How might you respond if someone were to ask you "What were you thinking about when you combined the _____ and the _____?

9. Invite students to create an ad for selling this new animal/instrument to their friends. Give students newsprint, crayons or markers, and the rule that the ad must picture the new creation and have no more than 10 words of copy. Refer to the "Ad Checklist" on page 56 for an assessment tool.

THE RUBRIC: GUITAR GATOR

Standard: Demonstrates ability to make forced relationships among familiar but unlike objects.

Criteria	1	2	3	4
Uses the Rules of Brainstorming	multiple and/or blatant rule breaker	breaks rules three to four times in activity	breaks rules one to two times	follows all rules during activity
Sketches Animal with Forced Relationships	sketches one with no relationship to the other	literal relationships	generic relationships	subtle connections
Creates Ad for New Animal	meets fewer than three check list indicators	creates literal connection	creates generic connections	creates clever and subtle connections
Explains Value of Forced Relationships	no valid reason	one valid reason	two valid reasons	multiple valid reasons

Tools: Check lists; What? So What? Now What?; student webs

Comments:

_____

_____

_____

Scale	
_____	= A
_____	= B
_____	= C
Below ___	= Not Yet

Final Grade: _____

The following tool may be used to evaluate the "Guitar Gator" ad:

AD CHECKLIST

- ❏ 16" x 24" or larger
- ❏ multiple colors
- ❏ few key words
- ❏ humor
- ❏ visual objects
- ❏ tied together
- ❏ neatness
- ❏ eye-catching
- ❏ makes a point
- ❏ uses an ad technique
- ❏ other

Scale
A = 9+
B = 7+
C = 5+
D = 3+

Note: Each item is worth one point.

Make Your Own

NAME(S)_____ DATE_____ TEACHER_____

PROJECT: _____

INTELLIGENCES: _____

STANDARDS: _____

PRODUCT: _____

"What did we learn?"

_____

_____

"Why is this important?"

_____

_____

"What will we do with what we learned?"

_____

_____

TARGETED INTELLIGENCES: _____

SUPPORTING INTELLIGENCES: _____

THINKING SKILLS: _____

SOCIAL SKILLS: _____

CONTENT FOCUS: _____

MATERIALS: _____

TASK FOCUS: _____

PRODUCT: _____

PROBLEM: _____

ACTIVITY: _____

_____

_____

_____

_____

_____

_____

_____

_____

_____

_____

_____

_____

_____

_____

REFLECTIONS: _____

_____

_____

_____

_____

_____

_____

_____

_____

_____

_____

THE RUBRIC

Standard:

Criteria	1	2	3	4

Tools:

Comments:

_____

_____

_____

Scale
_____ = A
_____ = B
_____ = C
Below ___ = Not Yet

Final Grade: _____

Teacher-made tests and quizzes

In traditional classrooms, teacher-made tests and quizzes are one of the few options to standardized tests. Before Scantron, teacher-made tests and quizzes were a common tool for assessing knowledge. After Scantron, teacher-made tests that required essay responses became nearly extinct. While such tests require time to correct, they remain a valuable alternative for assessing what students know about course content and the processes of learning.

The most helpful teacher-made tests prompt students to display their knowledge while responding to higher-order thinking prompts. The three-story intellect model (Bellanca and Fogarty, 1991) provides an easy-to-use reference for constructing challenging test questions in the middle and secondary grades. Many teachers keep this model handy when they are constructing written tests or giving surprise oral quizzes.

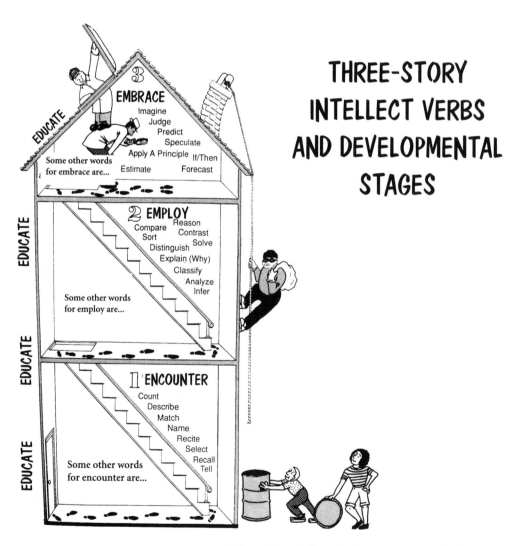

(Adapted from Bellanca & Fogarty, 1991. Used with permission.)

PRIMARY EXAMPLE

(Teacher ask questions and record responses.)

1. How many sides does each have?
    Triangle   _____
    Square   _____
    Circle   _____
    Rectangle   _____

2. What shapes do you see in this room?

3. Tell your favorite shape and explain why.

MIDDLE GRADE EXAMPLE

Topic: _Angles (Geometry) Quiz_
Intelligence: _Logical/Mathematical_

1. Define a right triangle in your own words.
2. Draw/label each of the following: an obtuse angle, a right angle.
3. Explain why you think it is important for any two of the following people to know their angles:
    (1) a hockey goalie
    (2) an architect
    (3) a surgeon
    (4) a student
4. Here is a problem involving a triangle. Write instructions for guiding a friend to solve it. Find the area of a right triangle with a base that is 5 feet long and a height of 10 feet. Keep in mind that the formula for finding the area of a right triangle is $\frac{1}{2}$ (base × height) = Area.

SECONDARY SAMPLE TEST

Topic: _Classification of Insects*_
Intelligence: _Logical/Mathematical_
Name: _Georgia Escalante_   Unit: _Insect Classification_
Instructor: _Mr. Kapheim_

1. Match the terms in column A with the definitions in column B.

A		B
a. Segmentation	_____	An external protective structure
b. Locomotion	_____	Radiating from a common center
c. Symmetry	_____	Division into segments
d. Exoskeleton	_____	Beauty as a result of balance
e. Radial	_____	Means of movement

2. Explain the term: to classify.

3. Here is a list of household objects. Classify them in at least three groups. Label each group and explain the common characteristics of each group.
    pen, knife, tablecloth, window, notebook, rug, wallpaper, pencil, door, lampshade, candle, book jacket, vent, table

4. Identify three occupations and explain why the ability to classify is important to each job.

Graphic organizers and designs

Graphic organizers not only help students learn how to learn as they work with information, these tools also help them structure assessments. In judging these assessments, the teacher can use the standards of fluency (how many items) and accuracy (the items fit the judgment).

Many of the basic graphic organizers lend themselves for use as assessments tools. To use one for assessment, first select the particular graphic organizer the students will use. Second, target what the students will assess (the standard? one or more criteria? the indicators of success?). Next, decide whether the students work alone or together on a particular assessment task. Finally, make sure that—before each student uses the selected graphic organizer/tool for assessment—he or she knows how it works.

PRIMARY EXAMPLE

Using a student in each group who can write, have the students construct a web showing all they have learned about a topic such as nutrition or problem solving. Give the fluency/accuracy performance criteria before they start (A =24 items, B=18, C= 12, etc.).

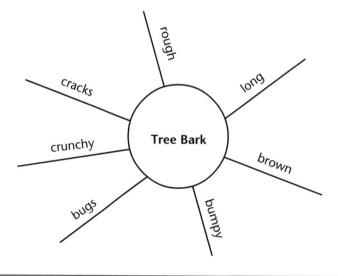

MIDDLE GRADE EXAMPLE

Topic: _Assessing Performance_

Intelligences: _Visual/Spatial, Logical/Mathematical_

Purpose: To enable students to assess themselves on a specific assignment by using a balance (a graphic organizer) to weigh the pros and cons of their performances.

Activity:

1. Have students view an illustration of a balance, a weighing device such as the one shown. You may show a reproduction of a balance using an overhead projector or you may just draw the scale on the chalkboard. Have students sketch their own balances for this activity.

2. Instruct students that they will use a balance to weigh the pros and cons of their performances on a particular learning assignment.

3. Assign a content-specific project (e.g., essay, book report, mathematical problem-solving task, science experiment) for this activity.

4. Create a rubric or review strategy for this project, such as the shown on page 59, showing the criteria and indicators of success: 1, 2, 3, and 4.

5. Give each student this rubric or check list so that they can rate their performances on the project, with each indicator of success being worth a weight of 5.

6. After each student has completed the project and review, scoring his or her performance using the rubric, the student should be instructed to draw symbols for all the indicators of success (scores), picturing them as "weights" in the left-side "pro/plus" dish of the balance. If a student did not attain an indicator of success for any one criterion, he or she should place that respective symbol in the "con/minus" dish on the right side of the scale.

7. After all indicators are placed on the balance, have each student calculate the total point score (remembering that each indicator is worth 5) and redraw his or her scale to show the balance—reflecting the student's performance on the project graphically. For example, if a student only met half the criteria, the scale would be evenly balanced. Have the students attach the drawing to their project reviews.

8. Check each student's performance evaluation rubric and go over his or her "balance," checking whether scores were calculated correctly and performance is reflected accurately on the balance.

SECONDARY EXAMPLE

Topic: _The Multiple Intelligences_
Intelligences: _Visual/Spatial, Intrapersonal_

Name: _Kate Hoffman_   Course: _Psychology I_   Date: _4/11_
Teacher: _Bob Applebaum_

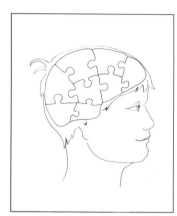

1. Outline a model head of a person. Divide it into eight parts.
    Make each part equal in size to the strength of each of your eight
    intelligences. Label the intelligence and give an example of how
    you use that intelligence.

2. Explain why you chose the _____ intelligences as your strongest.

3. Explain how you might improve your _____ intelligence.

Make Your Own

NAME(S)_____ DATE_____ TEACHER _____

PROJECT: _____

TARGETED INTELLIGENCE: _____

SUPPORTING INTELLIGENCES: _____

THINKING SKILLS: _____

SOCIAL SKILLS: _____

CONTENT FOCUS: _____

MATERIALS: _____

TASK FOCUS: _____

PRODUCT: _____

PROBLEM: _____

ACTIVITY: _____

_____

_____

_____

_____

_____

_____

_____

_____

_____

_____

REFLECTIONS: _____

_____

_____

_____

- - - - - - - - - - - - - - - - - - - **THE RUBRIC** - - - - - - - - - - - - - - - - - - -

Standard:

Criteria	1	2	3	4

Tools:

Comments:

_____

_____

_____

Scale
_____ = A
_____ = B
_____ = C
Below ___ = Not Yet

Final Grade: _____

A MAP TO THE MULTIPLE INTELLIGENCES

Verbal/Linguistic
The ability to use with clarity the core operations of language.

Musical/Rhythmic
The ability to use the core set of musical elements.

Logical/Mathematical
The ability to use inductive and deductive reasoning, solve abstract problems, and understand complex relationships.

Interpersonal
The ability to get along with, interact with, work with, and motivate others toward a common goal.

Visual/Spatial
The ability to perceive the visual world accurately and to be able to recreate one's visual experiences.

Intrapersonal
The ability to form an accurate model of oneself and to use that model to operate effectively in life.

Bodily/Kinesthetic
The ability to control and interpret body motions, manipulate physical objects, and establish harmony between the body and mind.

Naturalist
The ability to see similarities and differences in one's environment.

Chapman (1993, p. 197)

®SkyLight

Assessing Performances in Verbal/Linguistic Intelligence

What is verbal/linguistic intelligence?

Verbal/linguistic intelligence is the ability to use with clarity the core operations of language. Only human beings communicate through the written word. When we communicate through reading, writing, listening, or speaking, we are employing the significant components of this intelligence. More important, human beings can also link prior knowledge and understanding to new information and can explain how the linkage occurs. The verbal/linguistic intelligence that enables us to make our personal perceptions understood is probably one of the most important of the multiple intelligences in our culture. Verbal/linguistic intelligence helps the student produce and refine language use in its many forms and formats. The ability to form and recognize words and word patterns by sight, by sound, and for some by touch, is the start. After learning to read and write in the basic patterns, the more advanced learner learns to distinguish the many formats of language including stories, essays, and poems, and the techniques of language such as metaphor, hyperbole, symbol, and grammar. These are enriched with meaning by abstract reasoning, conceptual patterns, feeling, tone, structure, and an ever-expanding vocabulary. Ultimately, the peaks of language development are reached by those who combine sound and sense in unique patterns to express universal thoughts and to speak to the hearts of the many.

Why is verbal/linguistic intelligence important in the curriculum?

In today's fast-paced world of burgeoning information, the development of this intelligence is essential. The key to understanding the complexities of the technological and global aspects of life in the twenty-first century is well-developed verbal/linguistic intelligence. We work at developing language so that we can better understand one another. We use words to interpret feelings, actions, steps in a formula, and end results. Language, written or spoken, is our primary communication tool.

Therefore, it is mandatory that the curriculum provide opportunities for verbal/linguistic development. Students need to be as proficient in reading technical manuals as they are in reading fiction. They need to be able to express their understandings orally as well as in prose. The command of this intelligence assures success in the interpersonal interchanges that are the foundation of the human experience.

What classroom practices develop verbal/linguistic intelligence?

In a first grade classroom in Ohio, students are getting ready to study a unit on fish. Before they begin, they are instructed to think about what they know about fish. Each student creates a list of *words* describing what he or she already knows about fish. When all have created their lists, the teacher puts students in groups of three with a recorder in each group. The recorder makes a chart listing what the students in the group already know about fish and what they want to know. In this exercise the students recall their prior knowledge and develop language to enrich what they already know.

FISH	
Know	Want to Know

When the class has finished brainstorming, the teacher creates a chart for the class of what students already know about fish and what they want to know. The "what they want to know" becomes part of the unit of study and allows students to explore the issues they believe are relevant to their understanding of fish. They have used their verbal/linguistic intelligence to broaden their understanding of the topic.

In a tenth grade English class, students have just finished reading *The Scarlet Letter*. They work in groups of four to discuss a central character in the novel. Using a Venn diagram, the students discuss all the characteristics of Hester, a single parent in New England in 1642. They compare her to Murphy Brown, a single parent in Washington, D.C. in 1992. They consider the insightful similarities of these two fictional single mothers. As they discuss and fill in their graphic organizer, the Venn, they create an information base from which each will write a critical essay on the two fictional characters. They use their verbal skills to help them in the writing process. The teacher moves from group to group to monitor the discussions and encourage the verbal interchanges. Her most frequent questions are "why do you think that?" or "how do you know that is true?" as she encourages students to link prior knowledge gained from reading the book or seeing the television program to the characters' behaviors. Rather than tell students the answers, her questions encourage the students to develop their verbal/linguistic skills.

What standards could a teacher use to develop a rubric for verbal/linguistic intelligence?

Precision

The accurate use of language is one of the standards set to help students develop their verbal/ linguistic skills. Teachers watch for growth in vocabulary as students strive to enrich the spoken and written language they use to express themselves. As they develop an understanding of the nuances of words, students' writing becomes more precise.

Logic

The logic standard is set so that students are not carried away with the sound of words alone. Students are first asked to create the logic of a beginning, middle, and an ending. As they become more adept, they are asked to create oral or written pieces for a variety of audiences, to understand the logic of which information would be most meaningful to which audiences, and to demonstrate how they would deliver meaningful information to different audiences. From the logic of *sequence*, students learn to use formal logic by writing arguments, providing supporting evidence, and proving a point with examples.

Flexibility

The flexibility standard is set so that students become proficient in reading and writing in multiple ways. Students need to be as proficient in reading "how-to" manuals as in reading a novel. They need to experiment with a variety of reading and writing formats across the curriculum and to handle a number of different types of reading and writing assignments. Most importantly, they need to develop flexible thinking. As students examine a problem, they need to explore many possible answers to help them think about new arrangements.

What is a sample rubric for verbal/linguistic intelligence?

The rubric scale is determined with two considerations in mind: (1) which standard has been selected, and (2) the student's developmental level. The standard of precision, for example, will be very different for a second grade student than for a high school student. Sixth grade students would be expected to write in complete sentences, using capital letters and periods correctly. Eleventh graders would be expected to accurately explain an event or a problem-solving experience and to describe resolutions, as well as show basic precision in the correct use of punctuation.

MIDDLE SCHOOL (SIXTH GRADE)

- **THE RUBRIC** -

Targeted Standard: Language Precision

CRITERIA

High Performance: The student writes in complete sentences; uses all punctuation and capitals correctly; gives precise descriptions.

> **Indicators:**   All punctuation and capitalization are accurate.
> Descriptions are lengthy and extremely detailed.
> Sentences are complete and complex, showing much thought.

Sound Performance: The student writes in complete sentences; uses most punctuation and capitalization correctly; uses language in sentences to accurately describe a situation.

> **Indicators:**   Almost all punctuation and capitalization are accurate.
> Descriptions are lengthy and detailed.
> Sentences are complete and complex.

Adequate Performance: The student writes in complete sentences with some errors in punctuation and capitalization and provides brief descriptions of a situation.

> **Indicators:**   Most punctuation and capitalization are accurate.
> Descriptions are adequate and somewhat detailed.
> Sentences are complete but contain some errors.

Not Yet: The student does not write in sentences but can orally describe a situation with teacher cues.

> **Indicators:**   Punctuation and capitalization are not used.
> Descriptions are inadequate and lack detail.
> Sentences are very fragmented.

The rubric is set as a guideline for students. They need to be very clear in their understanding of the requirements before they even begin an assignment. They need to know what is meant, for example, by "complete sentence." To help students become successful in using this intelligence, teachers need to provide models of precise performance in the use of language.

Most of the time should be spent on explaining the high performance model. After reviewing the rubric, the teacher can distribute two or three high performance sample essays that meet the high performance criteria standard. Once students see and discuss what is expected and understand the steps to achieving the standard, they can work to accomplish it.

In today's schools, the verbal/linguistic intelligence gets the most use, especially for teachers who love to lecture and talk. Students need lots of talk time to develop their own verbal/linguistic intelligence. This applies not only to those with gifted tongues, but also to those who escape developing this intelligence by being shy and retiring. Human beings separate themselves from other animals through the ability to communicate with a complex system of words. Through dialogue and explanation, children develop their ability for communication and clear thought. As they discuss an idea or event, children increase the complexity of their own understanding about what they are saying and create a common ground for interacting with others.

What assessment tools are most useful for verbal/linguistic intelligence?

Teacher-made tests

The teacher-made test can be a powerful tool to evaluate a student's verbal/linguistic intelligence. Tests are not always limited to pen and paper. For young students who can't write or older students for whom writing is a physical challenge, the teacher or a volunteer may read the questions and use a tape recorder or check list for the response.

A primary teacher may use pictures to encourage a student to explain a sequence of events. As the teacher and student talk, the teacher asks the student to explain why the sequence was chosen. The teacher evaluates the student's ability for precision as they discuss the event or the sequence of a story. By using a video- or audiotape to capture the student's mastery of language, the teacher gives both parent and student a permanent record of achievement. The taping can be done at the beginning and end of the year to capture a student's growth in the use of language. Such taping does not have to be long; several minutes of a child's explanation are all that is needed for a benchmark.

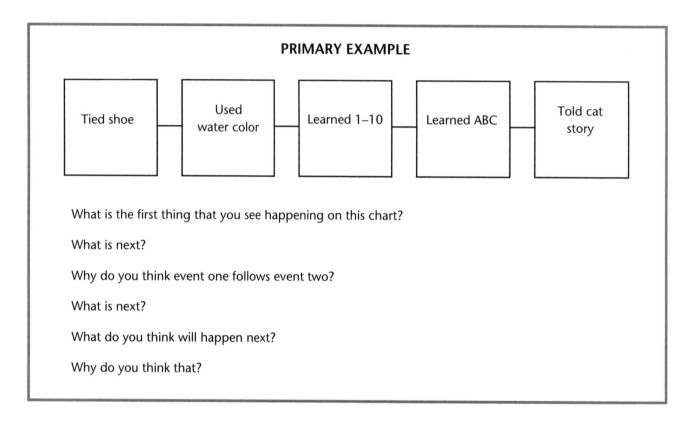

PRIMARY EXAMPLE

| Tied shoe | Used water color | Learned 1–10 | Learned ABC | Told cat story |

What is the first thing that you see happening on this chart?

What is next?

Why do you think event one follows event two?

What is next?

What do you think will happen next?

Why do you think that?

In the secondary classroom, there is ample opportunity to develop the verbal/linguistic intelligence with teacher-made essay tests.

Tests for older students need to go beyond recall to fill-in-the-blank and multiple-choice: A well-designed test includes at least one open-ended question. At each level of thought, the evaluation criteria should appear in the instructions (see Three-Story Intellect, p. vii).

SECONDARY EXAMPLE

Name_____   Date_____

This is an essay exam. Its purpose is to see (a) how well you can express your ideas in writing and (b) how precise you are in using correct grammar, spelling, and punctuation. On the bulletin board, reread our rubrics for "clarity" and "precision." Use these as guides for the quality of your answers.

1. *Describe* the event that you think most changed Hamlet's belief system.
2. If you were to change the plot resolution, what changes would you make? Explain how your change would change the play's ending. Provide reasons for your changes.
3. Think about what you have learned about personal decision making from this play. In what ways can these learnings benefit you in your daily life?

Demonstrations

Students have a variety of options for demonstrating their oral skill in the verbal/linguistic intelligence. They may select favorite movie scenes, situations from novels or plays, powerful political speeches, and historical events to demonstrate specific abilities, such as tone, emphasis, or interpretation.

For example, a teacher may look for his or her students' ability to replicate the language patterns appropriate to the situations being modeled. This is as true for first graders as it is for secondary students. In either situation, students are expected to use the idiomatic language of the people they are modeling.

Using a framework for the verbal demonstration, the teacher and the student discuss and agree on what verbal/linguistic behavior should be modeled. The student and the teacher set the criteria expected to be seen in the selected role-play. Together they establish:
- Purpose of the demonstration
- Verbal/linguistic characteristics expected to be demonstrated
- Student portrayal of the different verbal/linguistic structures

The student uses the selected vehicle (i.e., role-play, dramatic reading) and performs for a live audience or records his or her performance on audio or videotape. The teacher uses a check list of the criteria. For instance, in a dramatic reading of Poe's "The Raven," the check list might include appropriate facial gestures, arm movements, volume control for emphasis, and so on.

Group projects

Group projects that result in individual accountability are a very positive assessment tool for this intelligence. Students can glean the best thinking from their group partners and then translate this thinking into their own understanding. Together the group decides on its course of action—how to tackle the assignment, how to research it, how to formulate it, and how to present it. All these life-processing skills require a refinement of the verbal/linguistic intelligence. As students work together on any group project, they hone their verbal/linguistic skills. They talk together, and come to understand what they are all about and how they will put their combined ideas together for the rest of their classmates. Such interchange requires the practiced use of verbal/linguistic skills.

The teacher moves from group to group monitoring the group interaction, the level of problem-solving questions being asked, and the quality of the written group summary. Such monitoring provides the teacher with insight into the student's capability in verbal interactions. Teachers may use a group chart that identifies verbal behaviors used well.

CHECK LIST

Drama 202

Student Name _____ Date _____ Event _____

	Strong Demonstration	Good Demonstration	Not Yet
Strong voice projection			
Clear eye contact with audience			
Facial gestures fit feeling of text			
Appropriate gestures			
Multiple inflections			

Logs and journals

Students can also demonstrate their verbal/linguistic intelligence by writing in their journals or thinking logs about interchanges among their peers. As students reflect on classroom exchanges or the conversations that helped shape the group activities, they develop the skill of verbalizing on paper. They also link their insights about group interaction to insights about what constitutes positive group interaction. Early primary students can enter this process by drawing pictures and creatively writing key words about their understanding of the group dynamics. Middle grade and secondary students can reflect in writing about their group's interaction. Whatever the grade level, students need the time to reflect on the language learning that occurs in group interactions. When given the opportunity to write reflectively in logs or journals, students learn to translate the spoken word into prose.

The following suggested journal stems give students an opportunity to reflect about their own verbal/linguistic interactions with peers. Reflective journal entries give students the chance to monitor what was going on in their classroom interaction, what was said, and what it meant. Because the verbal/linguistic intelligence provides human beings with such a highly interactive communication skills, teachers should provide a variety of opportunities to develop this intelligence. The reflective journal is one strategy that encourages such development.

PRIMARY EXAMPLES

I like it best when my group. . . .
I know I am learning in my group when. . . .
I am successful when. . . .
When my group works together, I know that. . . .

MIDDLE GRADE EXAMPLES

Today my group helped me. . . .
One thing I learned from talking together is. . . .
The way I think the group works together best is. . . .

SECONDARY EXAMPLES

Group interaction makes it possible to. . . .
One thing I realize from group interaction is. . . .
I prefer to express myself by. . . .
When my group gets together, I realize. . . .

Observation check lists

Another way teachers can assess the verbal/linguistic intelligence is with observation check lists. Check lists help teachers measure the quality of the verbal interchange among students. Positive student interchange can be heard in situations that promote social skills growth or in activities that foster higher-order thinking skills development.

To make an observation check list, the teacher first decides what verbal/linguistic skill he or she expects from individuals (e.g., encouragement or higher-order questioning). Second, the teacher creates an observation check list including these skills. Third, the teacher lets students know the verbal cues that he or she is listening for during whole group instruction or in small groups. Examples of cues:

PRIMARY EXAMPLES

What a good idea!

Thank you for sharing that with me.

I like that idea.

What do you think?

Why do you think that?

Why do you think we should do it that way?

Explain the difference between the two. . . .

MIDDLE GRADE EXAMPLES

Tell me more about. . . .

That's a great idea because. . . .

Can you give some more detail?

How can we work on this together?

SECONDARY EXAMPLES

Explain how you see the difference between. . . .

What do you think would happen if. . . .

This seems to be similar to. . . .

The teacher, using an observation check list, moves from group to group, monitoring student interchanges and responses. The teacher listens to the student conversations to determine the amount of positive student interdependence and the quality of higher-order questions students ask. The observation check list keeps the teacher focused on evaluating the quality of the interactions students are developing. As instruction progresses, the teacher uses the check list to record the comments of individual students. (See the example on the following page.)

GROUP OBSERVATION CHECK LIST

Directions: Ask each member of the group to tally the number of times they see other group members using the targeted social skill.

Topic: _____ Date: _____

Class: _____ Teacher: _____

DIRECTIONS:

1. Select a social skill you plan to observe for one activity, one day, or one week.
2. Put a " ✓ " every time you observe your team members use the social skill.
3. Fill in the comments section below.
4. Share your observations and comments with your group members.

GROUP MEMBERS	TARGETED SOCIAL SKILL	MON.	TUES.	WED.	THURS.	FRI.	TOTAL
1.							
2.							
3.							
4.							

COMMENTS: _____

_____

_____

_____

_____

Burke (1993, p. 115)

Interviews

Interviews are one of the strongest techniques teachers use to develop the verbal/linguistic intelligence. A primary teacher may take the time to ask students individually, "What are your goals as a reader this year?" or "What kinds of stories do you like to read?" These questions focus students on the scope of their reading; what they are interested in; and what their reading/communicating goals are for the year.

Interviews provide an insightful opportunity to find out where the student believes he or she is as a reader and what his or her personal reading outcomes might be for the academic year.

PRIMARY EXAMPLES

James, what kinds of stories do you like to read?
What is your goal as a reader?
What kinds of things do you like to write about?
What would be a fun writing experience for you?

MIDDLE GRADE EXAMPLES

Rebecca, tell me about your reading habits.
What kind of letter writer are you? Explain.
What fictional character would you like to be and why?
What reading goals have you set for yourself this year?

SECONDARY EXAMPLES

Steve, tell me about your reading habits.
What kinds of books do you read for pleasure?
What kind of an essay writer are you?
What reading and writing goals have you set for yourself this year?

How do I align assessment with a lesson focusing on verbal/linguistic intelligence?

The following is a sample lesson and an assessment that focuses on verbal/linguistic intelligence.

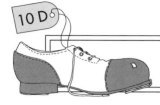

Sample Lesson: Verbal/Linguistic

Home Page

TARGETED INTELLIGENCE: Verbal/Linguistic

SUPPORTING INTELLIGENCES: Intrapersonal, Visual/Spatial

THINKING SKILLS: Problem solving, reviewing prior learning

SOCIAL SKILLS: Working in pairs

CONTENT FOCUS: Language arts/media communications

MATERIALS: Computers and appropriate software

TASK FOCUS: Students will create a Web page.

PRODUCT: Autobiographic home page (the first page of a Web site)

PROBLEM: How to write an autobiography on a home page

ACTIVITY:
1. Check students' prior knowledge of the genre "autobiography." Fill in with enough information so they can define the term.
2. Check students' prior knowledge of a home page/Web site. Identify major components that require written composition (ad copy, explanations, instructions).
3. Show the students a personal home page. You may refer them to the example on page 83 as a start or, better yet, create your own personal Web site/home page as an example. Include the following attributes:
   a. a catchy title
   b. a brief introduction that leads to "more"
   c. subheads to describe such areas as best characteristics, important life moments, personal time line, accomplishments, interests and hobbies, etc.
   d. a functional design and layout
4. Provide other criteria such as length, grammar, and sentence structure expectations.
5. Establish due dates for outline, first draft, and final product. Assign each student a partner.
6. Instruct each student to review his or her partner's home page and offer feedback.
7. Collect printouts, review, and provide your own feedback on completed home pages.

REFLECTIONS:
1. What did we learn about autobiographies and home page design?
2. How might we use these learnings in other classwork as well as outside of school?

THE RUBRIC: HOME PAGE

Standard: Designs a Web page based on his or her life story.

Criteria	1	2	3	4
Understands How an Autobiography Is Written	confuses autobiography with biography	identifies key attributes of an autobiography	identifies key attributes and other nuances of autobiography	differentiates with examples of types of autobiographies
Understands How to Make Home Page	no evidence of attributes	identifies key attributes of home page	identifies key attributes and quality benchmarks	describes key attributes and quality benchmarks on home page
Designs Home Page for Autobiographic Web Site	autobiographic element weak	blends key attributes of autobiography with home page	benchmarks for both elements met	shows exceptional creativity beyond benchmarks in final product
Assesses Quality of Autobiographic Home Page	no assessment done	assesses without structure	uses PMI with three to four examples per column	Uses PMI with five to seven examples per column

Tools: PMI; check list

Comments:

_____

_____

_____

Final Grade: _____

Scale
_____ = A
_____ = B
_____ = C
Below ___ = Not Yet

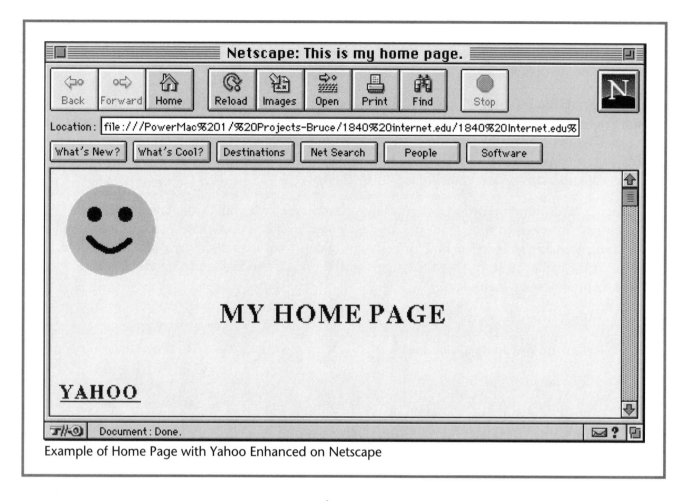

Example of Home Page with Yahoo Enhanced on Netscape

How can I assess verbal/linguistic intelligence when it is integrated across the curriculum?

Because language distinguishes human behavior and identifies the ability of humans to reason, the verbal/linguistic intelligence crosses all disciplines. It is also connected to the display of all the intelligences.

Aristotle defined humans as "rational animals." By this definition, he included humans in the "animal" genus because humans share such essential characteristics as warm blood and epidermal layers, and live-born offspring with other living creatures. These characteristics and other distinguished animals from insects, birds, and fish.

Aristotle's definition also distinguished the human species from the others in the animal genus by identifying the ability to reason as a unique and essential characteristic. The ability of humans to use a complex language system which includes classifiable words (nouns, adjectives, verbs) to construct and communicate meaning in an interactive way, to describe, to solve problems, and to argue or debate distinguishes humans from other animals such as lions, tigers, bears, gorillas, and dolphins.

Other animals communicate by simple sounds or signals that warn of danger, call for mates or young and establish direction. Even the dolphins signals are simple when compared to the complex structures and multiple uses of human language.

Human communication not only signals; it communicates the reasoning and meaning that human minds create. When two or more humans communicate, they process information using the agreed upon "sign" and symbol system, called words. Words establish a common ground for sharing and growing in understanding. When teachers teach using their verbal capabilities, they help students expand their verbal/linguistic intelligence.

Because verbal communication is so central to culture, the verbal/linguistic intelligence is commonly intertwined with all the other intelligences. In the multiple intelligences classroom, the skilled teacher's easiest method for helping students to develop their verbal/linguistic intelligence is the higher-order open-ended question that checks students' understanding and encourages them to develop their ideas.

> What would happen if . . .?
>
> How did you arrive at that idea?
>
> Why do you think that?
>
> What do you already know about . . . ?
>
> How is that like . . . ?
>
> How is that different from . . . ?

The oral or written response to such questions allows teachers to know where students are in their understanding of the curriculum as well as their skill level in the verbal/linguistic intelligence.

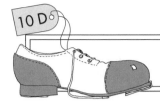

Sample Lesson: Verbal/Linguistic

Story Performance

TARGETED INTELLIGENCE: Verbal/Linguistic

SUPPORTING INTELLIGENCES: Intrapersonal, Interpersonal, Visual/Spatial

THINKING SKILL: Analysis

SOCIAL SKILL: Respect for others

CONTENT FOCUS: Analysis of "Three Billy Goats Gruff" or another children's story or fable; dramatics

MATERIALS: Several copies of the story to read, crayons/markers, 8 ½ × 11-inch poster-cards

TASK FOCUS: This activity involves the read aloud, the development of a mini-play, and a sharing with peers.

PRODUCT: Mini-plays (developed from a story)

PROBLEM: How to organize and develop content in a story

ACTIVITY:

1. Form groups of five. In each group, assign one student as a reader.

2. Have each group select its story—if you are providing choices. Make sure that the stories you provide have at least four roles. The reader will read the story aloud to the rest of the group. When he or she is done with this first read-through, the group will work together to make sure all members can retell the story—at least in an abbreviated manner.

3. Give the person sitting to the right of the reader five poster-cards. This person is assigned as the writer. The group will agree on who will play the roles in the story/mini-play, so that the group can eventually present the story to the class. With as much help as needed from the rest of the group, using the story as reference, the writer will print or write each of the story characters' names on the card. If there are only four characters in the story, one card may be an important object in the story. For example, in "Three Billy Goats Gruff" the roles would be the largest goat, the medium-sized goat, the little goat, the troll, and the bridge.

4. Give the groups time to plan and rehearse. Everyone should have a role to play in the mini-play, the "reader" or narrator (who tells the story during the performance) also being considered a role. Provide additional blank cards so the groups can label props for their mini-plays, if so desired. Encourage them to use important words from the story for such prop names ("river," as an example from "Three Billy Goats Gruff").

5. Allow the groups to present their mini-plays to the whole class.

6. After each mini-play is presented, encourage hurrahs and elicit comments from the audience—for instance, by saying "That is a wonderful story because . . . " Select one member of each performing group to tell you one way the team worked well together. Make a list of comments for all the groups on the chalkboard.

7. Finally, discuss with all the students how working together was important when they were preparing their mini-plays. What were some of the most helpful things they did together?

FOLLOW-UP

Use this reading/acting lesson in other subject areas. Have students act out math problems, how a plant grows, a historical event, a poem, or something else the class is studying. One member can read the study unit or instructions. The group can then create props and practice the performance.

THE RUBRIC: STORY PERFORMANCE

Standard: Presents a mini-play of a story.

Criteria	1	2	3	4
Each Student Will Agree Upon Story Roles in the Team	refuses to accept a role	passively accepts roles as agreed upon by others	participates in deciding roles	encourages and leads role selection
Students Will Rehearse Roles Together	disrupts rehearsal	passive participant	participates in helping others and learning own role	encourages and leads role rehearsal
Each Student Will Enact a Role	portrayal detracts from play	portrayal "fits in"	portrayal adds to success of play	portrayal is a "shining light"
Each Student Will Assess His or Her Contribution	one-word responses to Mrs. Potter's Questions	one-sentence responses to Mrs. Potter's Questions	multiple responses to at least one question	multiple and in-depth responses to all three questions

Tools: Mrs. Potter's Questions; observation chart

Comments:

_____

_____

_____

Final Grade: _____

Scale	
_____	= A
_____	= B
_____	= C
Below ___	= Not Yet

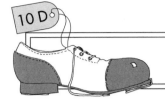

Make Your Own

TITLE: _____

TARGETED INTELLIGENCE: _Verbal/Linguistic_ _____

SUPPORTING INTELLIGENCES: _____

THINKING SKILL: _____

SOCIAL SKILL: _____

CONTENT FOCUS: _____

MATERIALS: _____

TASK FOCUS: _____

PRODUCT: _____

PROBLEM: _____

ACTIVITY: _____

_____

_____

_____

_____

_____

_____

_____

_____

_____

_____

_____

REFLECTIONS: _____

_____

THE RUBRIC

Standard:

Criteria	1	2	3	4

Tools:

Comments:

_____

_____

_____

Final Grade: _____

Scale

_____ = A

_____ = B

_____ = C

Below ___ = Not Yet

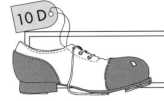

Reflection

Reflections on my assessment of verbal/linguistic performances:

What worked well in my classroom? _____

_____

_____

What would I like to change in my lesson and/or assessment of the lesson? _____

_____

_____

Where do I need help in improving this assessment? _____

_____

_____

What are other ideas I want to try for assessing this intelligence? _____

_____

_____

Notes: _____

_____

_____

_____

Ideas I want most to use:_____

_____

_____

_____

Assessing Performances in Musical/Rhythmic Intelligence

What is musical/rhythmic intelligence?

Musical/rhythmic intelligence is the language-related intelligence that starts with the degree of sensitivity one has to a pattern of sounds and the ability to respond emotionally to these sound patterns. As students develop pitch, tone, timbre, and rhythm, they develop this intelligence.

This intelligence has its own rules and thinking structures. These structures are not necessarily linked to other kinds of intelligence. Two common myths are that mathematical students make better musicians and that most musicians are better math students. The author of this chapter knows from her own experience that the second myth is definitely not true! She can sing but she cannot balance her checkbook! Children, more comfortable than adults with this intelligence, quickly learn words to jingles, raps, and complex songs even when reading or math skills are difficult for them. As they develop the intelligence, children may become adept at singing, playing a musical instrument, or dancing the ballet.

Musical/rhythmic intelligence is the acute awareness of sound in one's environment and the ability to use the core set of musical elements—pitch, rhythm, and tone.

Why is musical/rhythmic intelligence important in the curriculum?

In the MTV generation, music and its beats and rhythms are an important aspect of life. Yet, in our schools today, there is little classroom emphasis on the musical/rhythmic intelligence. Think about a high school parking lot before and after school. One of the first things a teenager does is turn on the radio to tune in to the beat. Videos and the sensational musical sound systems of today open up the world that students enjoy. Most children know the words to many popular songs and raps of today. Why is it they can learn all of this and not what we expect them to learn in the classroom?

Awareness of sounds is also a vital part of this intelligence, which emphasizes the auditory learning so important for all students. Special music classes, such as band, chorus, and glee club, are offered to very few students in the typical school. Generally, in a primary school, a student goes to music class thirty minutes once a week. In middle and secondary school, only those selected for a music class usually get to attend. With this selection process, the school system is telling many students they have no musical/rhythmic intelligence.

All classrooms should have planned musical/rhythmic activities so this intelligence can continue to grow in each student. Many of today's students, because of their extensive exposure to music, find this to be one of their favorite ways to learn.

What classroom practices develop musical/rhythmic intelligence?

An English teacher in Buffalo Grove, Illinois, has students writing songs, raps, poems, jingles, or cheers using important topics from the whole curriculum. After a group studies historical events or science principles, they create music to retell what they learned. Lyrics serve as an effective learning tool, because when they are trying to recall specific information, students recast ideas in verse with rhyme and beat. Their performances for the total class add much to the joy and celebration of learning.

A teacher from Florida insists on authentic sound in his biology projects. For example, when studying a unit on the rain forest, the students make a tape, re-creating the sounds of the rain forest.

Background music for some readers increases comprehension. A drafting teacher in Louisiana plays one of four pieces of classical music each time his high school drafting students work on their individual projects. At first, the students begged for more popular music. The teacher was persistent, however, and after a few months they would name the classical piece they wanted to hear while working. Many students felt they could not draw as well without the music.

What standards could a teacher use to develop a rubric for musical/rhythmic intelligence?

Originality

Music is a fine art. Its history is replete with scores that combine unique sounds and rhythms to please the ear. From simple songs to complex orchestrations, musical compositions make us laugh, cry, sing, and move. The originality standard applies to the young child who makes up a song; to the adolescent who seeks a new way to express his or her emerging feelings of love; and to the seasoned composer searching for a novel way to communicate powerful melodies. In all cases, the clue to originality is the different ways that a composer, young or old, arranges the rhythms and sounds of voice and instruments to create unique melodies that please the ear.

Accuracy

The young child practices rhythm and melodies at the piano, reading the score and coaxing his or her fingers to play as the score directs. How well he or she follows the symbols for speed, pitch, and beat tells how closely the child is following the songwriter's intent.

Comfort

Many learners believe they cannot achieve with the musical/rhythmic intelligence. Some are told "you're a frog" and are forced to sit out classroom practice while the "birds" sing. However, with the proper encouragement and training, most children rapidly acquire comfort with their own singing and rhythm.

Persistence

A persistent learner will not give up the task. When composing a song that won't rhyme, he or she sticks to the task, trying new combinations. When the dancer can't develop the precise movements to fit the music, he or she starts again. When the composer can't find an elusive sequence of notes, he or she begins again, perhaps working to the early morning hours. Over and over, he or she revises and edits in search of the perfect sound.

What is a sample rubric for musical/rhythmic intelligence?

In popular music, there are a great deal of repetitive and duplicated rhythms, scales, tones, words, and rhymes. The music that lasts beyond the popular fad avoids the fad and the quick success by being original. An original composition is one that contains novel sound arrangements.

THE RUBRIC: WRITING A SONG

Standard: Composes and performs a song about a story.

Criteria	1	2	3	4
Originality	substitutes a few words in a familiar song	duplicates the tune of a song, but uses own words	revises familiar tune; uses own words	completely original; does not replicate a familiar song
Rhythm and Rhyme	song has little rhythm and/or rhyme	song has some rhythm and/or rhyme	duplicates the rhythm/rhyme of a familiar song	composition has unique rhythm and rhyme
Conveys Tone and Feelings of Story	tells of an incident in the story	tells of a character in the story as well	somewhat conveys the story's tone and characterization	interprets the story; tone and feelings conveyed
Prepares and Performs a Song	prepares song, but doesn't perform it	sings song, but forgets words two or more times	sings song, but forgets words once	prepares and performs original song without faltering

Tools: Observation check list; test

Comments:

_____

_____

Final Grade: _____

Scale	
_____ = A	
_____ = B	
_____ = C	
Below ____ = Not Yet	

What assessment tools are most useful for the musical/rhythmic intelligence?

Check lists

So much of the development of this intelligence can be assessed through an observation check list. Two types of lists are possible: one for observing attitudes and feelings about music and rhythm and another for noting developmental changes.

OBSERVATION CHECK LISTS

Attitudes and Feelings

(teacher or peer)

1. Participates in musical/ rhythmic activities eagerly
2. Enjoys and responds to the beat
3. Willing to try musical/ rhythmic experiences

4. Likes music time

Attitudes and Feelings

(self)

1. I like it when we sing.

2. When my group performs to the beat, I feel good about participating.
3. Background music being played during independent work time helps me concentrate.
4. I use the (title) song or rap to help me remember the (facts).

DEVELOPMENTAL CHECK LIST

- Uses music or dance as a way to recall information
- Solves problems using the musical/rhythmic intelligence
- Plays an instrument
- Walks with a rhythmic walk
- While concentrating, raps object to a beat
- Moves a body part (e.g., taps toes) to a beat
- Identifies sounds
- Responds to sound and beat
- Comprehends what is read during independent reading time with background music being played

Audiotapes and videotapes of performances

A student playing an instrument or singing could be taped performing several examples of his or her favorite or best-performed selections. The teacher or the student could choose these examples, which could be put on a tape, to show progress over a long period of time. For example, a monthly recording would show progress and improvement from month to month.

Tapes could also be used for total class or group performances, with curriculum-based songs, raps, jingles, cheers, or chants.

Anecdotal observation

"Anecdotal" notes about this intelligence are easily prepared and placed in the student's folder (adhesive notes are a convenient tool).

When the teacher observes a noteworthy experience that identifies a student's musical strengths or weaknesses and shows progress or "backsliding," he or she writes down on an adhesive note the dates, the student's name, and the significant event. The teacher adds details so he or she can look at it at a later date and know what was meant. After making the note, the teacher sticks it in the student's folder.

How do I align assessment with a lesson focusing on musical/rhythmic intelligence?

The following is a sample lesson and rubric that focuses on musical/rhythmic intelligence.

Sample Lesson: Musical/Rhythmic

Writing a Jingle

TARGETED INTELLIGENCE: Musical/Rhythmic

SUPPORTING INTELLIGENCES: Interpersonal, Verbal/Linguistic

THINKING SKILLS: Synthesis, decision making, creative recall

SOCIAL SKILLS: Consensus, interdependence

CONTENT FOCUS: Using songs to review course information

MATERIALS: Paper, pencils, pens, newsprint, markers, recordings

TASK FOCUS: Students in cooperative groups create jingles that review key concepts from a lesson.

PRODUCT: A jingle

PROBLEM: How to write a jingle that will review a lesson

ACTIVITY:
1. After completing a unit or lesson on any subject matter, introduce the jingle as a review tool.
2. Next, select two or three television or radio (advertising) jingles to play for the class.
3. Ask the class to establish the criteria for an effective jingle. List these criteria on newsprint for future reference.
4. Form trios. Instruct each trio to spend the class period agreeing upon the key information learned in the lesson. They may want to use a concept map or a matrix for this task. Let them know that the information gathered will be the content of a jingle they will create.

5. In the next class period, each trio will select the jingle for the group's use—rewriting the lyrics to a jingle with which the members are familiar or writing a jingle to their own original tune. The new lyrics should cover key information from the lesson. The finished jingle will essentially be an advertisement for the key concepts the group has learned.

6. Coach the teams as needed. Encourage the teams to use the established criteria as a guideline as they finalize the words and tunes of their jingles.

7. Have each trio present its jingle to the class at the conclusion of the unit.

8. Use the jingle as a review tool for middle and high school students.

9. Use as a motivator to encourage students to focus on the lesson's key concepts.

THE RUBRIC: JINGLE

Standard: _____ (varies with subject matter).

Criteria	1	2	3	4
Recall of Content	80% of content of lesson	85% of content of lesson	90% of content of lesson	95% of content of lesson
Rhyme	jingle doesn't rhyme	jingle rhymes, but wording is awkward	jingle rhymes; wording is original	jingle rhymes; wording is "catchy"
Rhythm	jingle has little or no rhythm	jingle has rhythm, but inconsistent	jingle has consistent rhythm	jingle's rhythm is "catchy" and tune is original

Tools: Test; observation check list

Comments:

_____

_____

_____

Final Grade: _____

Scale

_____ = A

_____ = B

_____ = C

Below ___ = Not Yet

How can I assess musical/rhythmic intelligence when it is integrated across the curriculum?

Because so many districts are working with short funds, music and other fine arts classes are the first to be cut. Thus, it is imperative that students are encouraged to develop this intelligence with music and rhythm integrated across the curriculum.

Sometimes it is *not* necessary to assess this intelligence when it is integrated into content lessons. When songs are used to teach content (i.e., the parts of speech, coins, algebraic rules), assessment of the content is different. How well did students master the skill?

At other times, assessing this intelligence is helpful. Students tend to develop the musical/rhythmic intelligence when they know that they will be assessed on their musical performances. This is accomplished by using one rubric for each intelligence integrated in the lesson. Thus, an algebra lesson (mathematical/logical) that ends with each student pair (interpersonal) writing a rap song (musical/rhythmic) that includes all the rules for a function should have one rubric for each intelligence.

Sample Lesson: Musical/Rhythmic

Musical Interview

TARGETED INTELLIGENCE: Musical/Rhythmic

SUPPORTING INTELLIGENCES: Logical/Mathematical, Interpersonal

SOCIAL SKILLS: Consensus-seeking, listening

CONTENT FOCUS: Knowledge of music in society; popular culture

MATERIALS: Large piece of newsprint, markers

TASK FOCUS: Students interview a musician to analyze the impact of music on society.

PRODUCT: Newspaper articles

PROBLEM: How to identify the ways music is used in society

ACTIVITY:

1. Let the students know the purpose of this lesson is to deepen their knowledge of music and its impact on the individual and society. Discuss how they think music can improve their quality of life. Arrange for a musician—professional, amateur, or student—to come to class for an interview.

2. Provide each student with the following interview questions, which reflect the four W's and the H—the five questions in the traditional journalistic model:
   a. Who are you? What do you do as a musician? Which instrument(s) do you play? Where, when, and why do you play?
   b. What specific music has most influenced your life?
   c. How has music in general influenced your life? What benefits has music brought to your life?
   d. What role does music play in our society?

3. Introduce the class to the musician. Designate three students, ahead of time, to ask the interviewee the questions listed above. Encourage follow-up questions from all of the students in the class. Have students take their own notes during the interview, advising them that they will be expected to write their own newspaper articles based on the interview.

4. After the interview, show students how to summarize and organize their notes, as well as how to structure their news articles, by using the following Newspaper Model as a graphic organizer.

5. After the students organize their information, they should write their articles in the inverted-pyramid style, starting with an opening statement (paragraph) of basic factual materials about the interview and following up with descriptive paragraphs (at least one elaborating on each major question in the following Newspaper Model). Finally, the students should write headlines for their articles.

6. Collect and assess the completed newspaper articles.

7. Provide generic feedback for the strengths and weaknesses of the interview articles. Use a T-chart as an organizer to highlight the points.

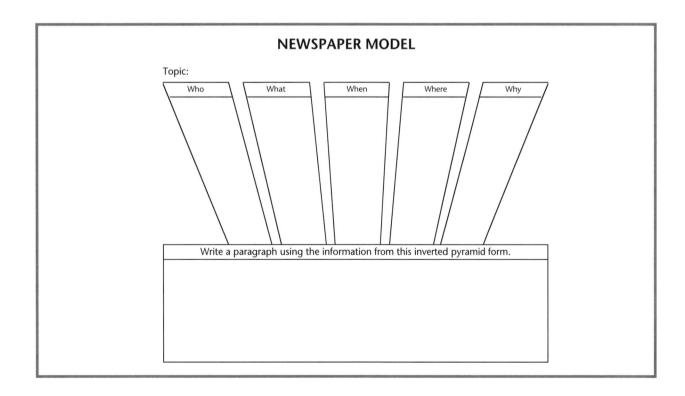

THE RUBRIC: MUSICAL INTERVIEW

Standard: Prepares a newspaper article based on a group interview with a musician.

Criteria	1	2	3	4
Collaborated in the Interview Process	individualistic behavior	followed the group interview format	active and equal collaborator in interview	coordinated the interview with equal time to all
Created a Well-Organized Article on the Musician's Ideas	random organization, model not followed	some pieces reflect the pattern in the model	answers the five key questions in the model	spirited responses to the model
Strong Descriptions	fuzzy	one to two sensory details	three or more sensory details	sensory details create feeling
Grammar, Syntax, and Structure Are Correct	seven or more errors	five to seven errors	two to four errors	one error or none at all

Tools: Check list

Comments:

_____

_____

_____

Final Grade: _____

Scale	
_____	= A
_____	= B
_____	= C
Below ___	= Not Yet

Make Your Own

TITLE: _____

TARGETED INTELLIGENCE: _Musical/Rhythmic_ _____

SUPPORTING INTELLIGENCES: _____

THINKING SKILLS: _____

SOCIAL SKILLS: _____

CONTENT FOCUS: _____

MATERIALS: _____

TASK FOCUS: _____

_____

PRODUCT: _____

PROBLEM: _____

ACTIVITY _____

_____

_____

_____

_____

_____

_____

_____

_____

_____

REFLECTIONS: _____

_____

_____

THE RUBRIC

Standard:

Criteria	1	2	3	4

Tools:

Comments:

_____

_____

_____

Final Grade: _____

Scale
_____ = A
_____ = B
_____ = C
Below ___ = Not Yet

Reflection

Reflections on my assessment of musical/rhythmic performances:

What worked well in my classroom? _____

_____

_____

What would I like to change in my lesson and/or assessment of the lesson? _____

_____

_____

What help do I need in improving this assessment? _____

_____

_____

What are other ideas I want to try for assessing this intelligence? _____

_____

_____

Notes: _____

_____

_____

_____

Ideas I most want to use: _____

_____

_____

_____

Assessing Performances in Logical/Mathematical Intelligence

What is logical/mathematical intelligence?

Logical/mathematical intelligence is the ability to use inductive and deductive reasoning, solve abstract problems, and understand complex relationships of mathematical reasoning and the scientific process. The critical thinking skills of sequencing, analyzing, and estimating are already embedded in most school curricula, but persistence, precision, inquiry, and elaboration need to be stressed more often. Teachers should use instructional approaches that will bring these to the forefront of classroom time and student use.

Beginning with the Greek philosophers, especially Aristotle and Plato, western civilization has given primary attention to the development of this intelligence. Some western cultures such as Germany have highly refined the logical/mathematical intelligence in science and engineering. Germany's thirteen-grade curriculum emphasizes rigorous mathematical training.

American schools give the most attention to the logical/mathematical intelligence, at least when it comes to standardized testing. Schools emphasize using inductive and deductive reasoning, solving abstract problems, and understanding complex relationships so that the individual can develop products based on mathematical reasoning and use those products with skill.

The logical aspects of this intelligence are built on deductive and inductive reasoning models. Each has a large set of rules to govern the right processes of thinking. From these two models have sprung applied systems of thinking including the scientific process, aeronautical engineering, and space technology.

Why is logical/mathematical intelligence important in the curriculum?

In a high-tech global society, the rationale for this intelligence is clear. Week after week, news stories describe layoffs of clerical and management workers whose jobs have given way to the computer. In manufacturing plants around the world, robots replace the assembly line. Those few individuals who survive the downsizing and rightsizing must learn how to work with new computer-dependent tools to do their jobs. This means they must think at complex levels as they analyze data, interpret information, and solve problems.

Mathematical reasoning and logic skills are critical. Secretaries, pipefitters, auto assemblers, army tank team members, medical technologists, and Ph.D. candidates in physics are required to use the logical/mathematical intelligence to a high degree in their daily work. A curriculum that neglects the development of this intelligence in any student is creating a major impediment to that student's ability to work and live in the high-tech world.

What classroom practices develop logical/ mathematical intelligence?

In a second grade classroom in Michigan, the teacher captures the attention of her thirty-two students seated at tables of four. She tells them that they are going to work on improving their math problem-solving skills. After she reviews their cooperative learning tasks, she gives each group a set of three, shoebox-sized blocks, a yardstick, and a hand calculator. She presents this problem: They are to discover how many of the blocks they will need to complete a wall from the front of the room to the back that is four blocks high. After checking for understanding, she walks among the groups to give help and encouragement, but no answers. When all groups are finished, she gathers the students together and asks a series of reflective questions. First, she wants to know how each group thought its way through the task. She hears many different methods. Next, she wants to know what they found easy and hard in solving the problem. Finally, after celebrating the skilled problem solving, she asks each group to tell how it might improve its thinking on the next task.

In a high school geometry class, the students see several pieces of rope of different lengths hanging from the ceiling. Each piece is weighted with a different object. When class begins, the teacher asks the students to "bet" which rope will swing the highest. The teacher reviews the acronym: "B=Base your prediction on fact"; "E=Estimate by calculating"; "T=Test your prediction." In small groups, students decide how to proceed and follow "BET." Some weigh the weights and measure the ropes' lengths. Others measure the swing from one member's push. When all the discussion is finished, the teacher asks each group to describe its prediction, show calculations, and demonstrate its tests. As ideas are put forth by the students, the teacher's most usual responses are "Why do you think that?" and "Show us your proof."

What standards could a teacher use to develop a rubric for logical/mathematical intelligence?

Problem solving

No standard seems more talked about and more ignored in practice for most students than the problem-solving standard. This standard calls for the math teacher to determine how well students can analyze a problem, develop a workable plan or system to solve the problem, and evaluate the plan's success after actually solving the problem.

Precision

The precision standard enables the teacher to determine how accurate and detailed a student can be in the application of a performance standard. For example, in science, did the student weigh each chemical to the exact decimal called for in the standard? In math, how accurate was the student in performing all calculations?

Accuracy

Accuracy is a critical standard in mathematics and science. In applied accounting classes, students may work against the standard of 100 percent accuracy in the computation of payables and receivables. In chemistry, measurements by weight (moles) are marked against a standard. How well does the student use this technique each time it is needed?

Metacognition

Metacognition refers to knowledge about, awareness of, and control over one's thinking processes. As a standard, metacognition is the ability to plan, monitor, and assess how one thinks through a task or problem. In a primary classroom, the standard marks the amount (quantity) and degree (quality) of student metacognition. For instance, the criterion might read: "Each time the student approaches a math problem-solving task, the student reviews what he or she already knows about that type of problem and notes what additional knowledge is needed before he or she can begin." In the middle grades, a mathematical metacognitive criterion might read: "The student asks purposeful prediction questions about the problem's solutions and tests the responses."

Logic

The logic standard helps the teacher assess the quality of the student's reasoning skills. How well does the student apply the rules of logic to solve a mathematical problem? A nonmathematical problem? In a debate, how free of bias is the argument? When using examples to support a point, do the student's examples align with the points being contended?

Transference

The transference standard is very important in the use of the logical/mathematical intelligence. It is not enough for the student to know the rules of math or logic. Transference means the student can apply these rules in other subject areas and outside the classroom. For instance, can the student apply logic rules learned for writing a coherent essay to the analysis of an editorial or the speech of a local politician?

What is a sample rubric for logical/mathematical intelligence?

Most major reports on the improvement of mathematics, including the call for new standards from the National Council of Teachers of Mathematics, identify problem solving as a critical area of learning for all students. In all grades, the standards for problem solving can take many forms. For instance, in the primary grades, standards can call for students to use a system or plan to solve a concrete mathematical problem. In the upper grades, the same standard can be modified for use in solving a geometry problem. Another standard might call for the student to trace how he or she solved the mathematical problem and explain certain procedures.

Once a standard is selected, the next step is to pick the appropriate criteria for success. The criteria need to align with the standard. In the case of a logical sequence chart-making problem, the standard for making a plan or system would have criteria which would serve as benchmarks, indicating the degree to which the student attains that standard. Note how these benchmarks indicate different degrees of success in the rubric on page 109.

To guide the students, the rubric may also contain a list of indicators which detail problem-solving behaviors. The indicators work best when they align with the standard and its criteria. For instance, for the planning standard, the rubric could detail such indicators as "writes out a sequence chart for each problem," "checks off each step done in each problem," "uses chart to guide accuracy check of each step" and "reviews the sequence of steps."

What assessment tools are most useful for logical/ mathematical intelligence?

For the rubric to have its most positive effect on student learning, it is important that the assessment tools align with the standards and criteria of the rubric. In the logical/mathematical intelligence, a rubric sets a standard on problem solving and sets up assessment tools that measure student problem-solving performances as well. If the teacher is also using an accuracy standard, the selected assessment tools should measure how accurately the student calculates. The tools discussed on the following pages were selected as the most appropriate options for assessing mathematical problem solving.

THE RUBRIC: LOGICAL SEQUENCE

Standard: Creates, defends, and transfers a sequence chart that shows a step-by-step plan.

Criteria	1	2	3	4
Plan for Chart	no evidence	two to three steps missing or out of order	one to two steps do not fit	all steps flow into each other
Defense of Chart	no rationale or evidence	can defend order of steps with a reason	can defend each step with a reason	can defend each step with a reason and examples
Transfer of Concepts	no uses demonstrated	can duplicate two or more points	can replicate	can create unique uses

Tools:

Comments:

_____

_____

_____

Final Grade: _____

Scale
_____ = A
_____ = B
_____ = C
Below ____ = Not Yet

Teacher-made tests

The teacher uses the teacher-made tests to assess students' knowledge and application of math concepts, skills, and information in a lesson or unit. The test questions should align with the standards for the logical/mathematical intelligence. For example, to measure problem-solving ability the test must check (a) knowledge about how to solve the mathematical problem, (b) the student's ability to solve several math problems at different levels of difficulty, and (c) the student's ability to write instructions on how to solve a given problem.

Since a math lesson or course may have several standards, the teacher-made test must balance the test items to reflect all the identified standards. For instance, if the course's second standard is precision, the teacher-made test should advise the students about how the precision criterion will be used in grading the test. The problems or math tasks given should provide opportunities for the students to show their precision as well as to solve the math problems.

PRIMARY EXAMPLE

Name: _____   Date: _____

1. Read the problem.

   Three students from the Jones School walked to school. Each came a different way. Mary walked three blocks. Dina walked nine blocks. Terry walked five blocks. What was the total number of blocks walked by the three students?

2. Make a plan. Tell the steps you will take to solve this problem after you have read it.

   ☐ — ☐ — ☐ — ☐ — ☐

3. Follow your steps and find the answer.

4. In a paragraph, explain what steps were easiest for you to do and why.

Demonstrations

In a demonstration, students model or show how to do a task. Like a television cook who demonstrates how to prepare a special meal or like a football coach who shows how to tackle and block, the student who models the logical/mathematical intelligence shows the teacher, the class, and the parents how to do a mathematical task. In the primary grades, the teacher might ask the student to show how he or she would arrange blocks in an a-b-b-a pattern. In middle grades, the student may show how to estimate the circumference of a water glass without a tape measure. In a high school class, the student might show how to measure the diameter of a triangle using three sticks. When these "demonstrations" are done in the context of a standard (e.g., the logical sequence rubric on page 109) and when the students must explain what they are doing and why (in mathematical terms that match the indicators in the rubric), they are a powerful assessment tool for this intelligence.

To assess a demonstration, the teacher can use a check list keyed to the rubric. A demonstration check list keyed to the problem-solving and accuracy standards might look like this:

Student Name: _____ Class: _____ Date: _____

___ explained purpose of demonstration

___ explained steps in demonstration

___ made accurate calculations

___ showed each step

___ explained reasons for each step

___ explained difficulties

Using a preestablished code, the teacher or other student observers complete the check list. As soon as the demonstration is finished, the observers give the student the check lists. If there are items not checked, the teacher discusses these with the student before the student puts the check lists into the portfolio.

Group and individual projects

Projects completed by cooperative groups and tested for individual accountability are a practical assessment tool. The students learn together in the project, but are assessed individually. For instance, middle grade math students work to solve spatial relations problems in a group. Each group is given a set of materials and a problem description card. The card asks the group to cut and fold rectangles that represent car seats. They cut circles to represent people. The card describes in words where each person sits in relation to other people or parts of the car. The object is to agree on where each person sits by using the rectangles and circles. After each group explains its reasoning to the class and the teacher checks for understanding, the teacher gives a new set of materials to each student. Assessment is made (a) on the results and the thinking processes used in the group problem-solving project and on (b) each student's ability to complete a similar problem-solving project on his or her own.

As with demonstrations, it is important that the students review the standard, the criteria, and the indicators before they start the problem and as they are working through it. A Likert scale, as shown on page 112, can give immediate feedback.

Group Members:_____   Date:_____

1. Analyzed the problem

----

no   sort of   yes

Observed evidence:

2. Made a plan

----

no   sort of   yes

Observed evidence:

3. Used the plan

----

no   sort of   yes

Observed evidence:

After the groups practice, receive feedback, and discuss how they might change their approaches to the problem, the teacher assigns each student an individual problem. As the students work, the teacher walks among the students and checks the scales. As each student completes the individual word problem, the teacher attaches the assessment scale to the final work.

Logs and journals

Math and science logs or journals provide a useful assessment tool for this intelligence. Because these tools give the students an opportunity to think about their mathematical and logical thinking, they are useful for promoting students' reflection about the problem-solving processes they are learning. Structured journal assignments before, during, or after the mathematical task enable the students to reflect on and to assess their own work. Stems, lead-ins, or structured questions that promote metacognition and are tied to the focus standards are useful starters for student thinking.

PRIMARY EXAMPLES

Before I start a word problem, it helps that I. . . .
I can help my math planning by. . . .
In math, I like to think about. . . .
In science, I plan best when I. . . .
Today, I learned. . . .
I can get better at math by. . . .

MIDDLE GRADE EXAMPLES

What I know about this problem is. . . .
What I did well in solving this problem. . . .
I can improve my math problem solving by. . . .
I think my strengths in math are. . . .

SECONDARY EXAMPLES

The steps to take in problem solving are. . . .
My strengths in math problem solving are. . . .
I am most logical when. . . .
I need to improve _____ in math because. . . .
Ways I can apply my math knowledge are. . . .

Interviews

Interviews take many forms in the math and science classrooms. The teacher can interview the student and students can interview each other or their parents. The first key to the successful assessment interview is its focus on the math and science knowledge and the attitudes of students to math and science. The second key is asking the right questions. The questions will fall into two categories: starter and extending. As the interviewer listens to the responses, he or she attempts to hear how well the student's responses fit with the performance criteria. For instance, if the interview is on a topic in earth science and the teacher is assessing for transfer of mathematical problem-solving skills to an earth science issue, the questions might sound like this:

Starter: Maria, what have you learned about solving problems in math that you can use to solve the problem of graffiti in the neighborhood? (Here the teacher listens for how well Maria analyzes the problem, explores alternative solutions, and chooses the solution which would have the most positive impact. However, the teacher also wants to hear how Maria intends to attack the problem. Will she outline the steps in problem solving? Will she make a plan? How systematic is Maria's approach?)

With a rubric in her hand or head, the teacher listens to Maria's answers and jots down her assessment on a check list or Likert scale.

How do I align assessment with a lesson focusing on logical/mathematical intelligence?

Following are a sample lesson and an assessment that focuses on logical/mathematical intelligence.

Sample Lesson: Logical/Mathematical

Measuring Everyday Objects

TARGETED INTELLIGENCE: Logical/Mathematical

SUPPORTING INTELLIGENCES: Interpersonal, Intrapersonal, Naturalist

THINKING SKILLS: Analysis, relationships

SOCIAL SKILLS: Communicating, listening, following directions

CONTENT FOCUS: Circumference measurement

MATERIALS: Overhead projector, five average drinking glasses (different sizes), paper plates (round, three different sizes), plastic bags, note cards, tape measures, and compasses (measuring instruments)

TASK FOCUS: This hands-on activity will help students understand the principles and procedures for measuring circumference.

PRODUCT: Completed algorithms, steps or rules followed to solve problems

PROBLEM: How to solve a circumference problem

ACTIVITY:

1. Define the following key terms, which will be used throughout this lesson: circumference, diameter, radius, and height.

2. Invite a student to place a drinking glass on the overhead projector and answer the question: Which is greater—the height of the glass or its circumference? Repeat this step until a total of five different students have answered the question/made their predictions for the five glasses.

3. Have each student measure the height and circumference of his or her glass using a measuring tape. On the chalkboard or on an overhead, create a chart for reporting the students' findings and record the height and circumference for each glass—as each student announces his or her results.

4. Ask the class to look at the results on the chart. Call on a randomly selected student to answer this question: What generalization can you make about which is greater—the height or the circumference of the glasses? (Note: The circumference is always larger.)

5. Now have each of the five students measure the diameter of his or her glass. Record this measurement on the chart as well (next to height and circumference) for each of the five glasses.

6. Next, ask each of the five students to divide the circumference of his or her glass by the diameter. Record the results on the chart next to the diameter for each of the five glasses.

7. Show that the results of the calculations done for step 6 are identical for all five glasses. Explain to the class that this value, circumference divided by diameter, is a constant: pi (= 3.14159).

8. Explain to the class that to find the circumference of any circle they may use the following formula: C = d. (Circumference equals pi multiplied by diameter.) Students will use this formula for the next part of the activity, measuring paper plates.

9. Divide the class into heterogeneous groups of three for the plate-measuring activity, giving each group a plastic bag that contains a note card, a tape measure, a compass mounted with a pencil, and three paper plates of different sizes.

10. Instruct each group that its job is to check the formula given in step 8, having each member of the group measure the diameter and circumference for one of the plates and then use the formula C = d to calculate circumference.

11. Have each student in the group compare his or her measurement of the circumference of the paper plate with the calculated value according to the formula above. (The results should be the same.)

12. Coach each student to mastery before giving the class a set of three word-problems on circumference to figure without using any concrete objects—giving each student a worksheet for guided practice. Be sure all the students understand the procedures and principles of the lesson before they start their individual worksheets.

13. Test for vocabulary, procedure, and the individual ability to solve several algorithms without guidance. Use the following rubric.

THE RUBRIC: MEASURING EVERYDAY OBJECTS

Standard: Defines key terms and demonstrates the use of each term in the solution of a circumference problem.

Criteria	1	2	3	4
Defines Terms	one or 0 correct (1)	50% correct (2)	75% correct (3)	100% correct (4)
Details Steps in Procedure	recalls less than 75%	recalls 80% of steps	recalls all steps	recalls all steps in sequence
Uses Procedure to Solve Algorithms	solves one or more	solves two algorithms	solves two algorithms and explains work	solves three high-level algorithms and explains work

Tools: Test; check list

Comments:

_____

_____

_____

Final Grade: _____

Scale	
_____	= A
_____	= B
_____	= C
Below ___	= Not Yet

How can I assess logical/mathematical intelligence when it is integrated across the curriculum?

Logic and math may be integrated across the curriculum in a variety of ways. For instance, in the primary grades, students may work on a project that challenges them to research their home town's history, interview important citizens, write a story about the town, and draw a scaled map of the town. In preparing the scale, the students must do measurements and accurate calculations. To assess this integrated unit, the teacher uses several standards. Each aligns with one of the intelligences developed in the project. From the logical/mathematical intelligence, the teacher selects problem solving, accuracy, or spatial reasoning. In the middle grades, the teacher elects to use a "threaded" model (Fogarty, 1991) for integrating mathematical reasoning across the curriculum. He or she develops the mathematical reasoning standard and the success criteria so that the tasks and activities from other intelligences match. Thus, in language arts, students use estimating skills to measure distances traveled by characters in a story (e.g., *Swiss Family Robinson*) or to draw a map of the scene (e.g., *The Most Dangerous Game*). In science, the students do accurate computations to contrast different weights of objects in and out of water. In social studies, the students use logic to debate two sides of an issue, such as raising/lowering taxes in the community.

In a secondary English classroom, the teacher uses the model in a unit on "tragic heroes." Groups of students prepare mock trials of Oedipus, Willy Loman, and Macbeth. Each group writes a brief either defending or prosecuting the main character for his mistreatment of his family. The logic rubric is applied to their legal briefs.

Sample Lesson: Logical/Mathematical

Measurement Magic

TARGETED INTELLIGENCE: Logical/Mathematical

SUPPORTING INTELLIGENCES: Bodily/Kinesthetic, Interpersonal, Visual/Spatial

THINKING SKILLS: Analysis, synthesis

SOCIAL SKILLS: Listening, accepting differences

CONTENT FOCUS: Metric conversion (distance measurement)

MATERIALS: Index cards, crayons or markers, measurement charts (English—traditional U.S.—and metric systems), newsprint, pencils

TASK FOCUS: Students master the process of converting metric to English measurements for distance.

PRODUCTS: Maps that contrast the distance measurement systems

PROBLEM: How to convert from metric to English measurements for distance

ACTIVITY:
1. Display the two measurement charts and ask the students to tell what they know about the words (i.e., foot, kilometer, etc.).
2. Identify what vocabulary they do *not* know and indicate that they must learn these words so they can convert one system (metric) into the other (English).

3. Divide the class into heterogeneous groups of three. In each group, assign roles (checker, reader, scorer).

4. Have each group divide the unknown vocabulary equally. Using the displayed charts, each person will write each unlearned term and its definition on an index card. On the opposite side, the person will write the conversion term.

5. Using the cards, the groups will do "teach arounds." After each three words, the checker "checks" the definition and conversion. Presentations and checks continue until all words are done. The checker ends with a check in the group of all words.

6. After all groups are done, each group will make a map using the metric system. The map must include at least one example of each measurement factor (i.e., meter, kilometer, etc.). It is appropriate to show examples "to prime the pump."

7. When the maps are done and signed by the creative team, exchange maps among groups. The new group must convert the measurements to the English system.

8. Check that all conversions are correct. Where necessary, reteach and clarify terms and conversions.

9. Give each student an individual map you have made with metric measurements. Students will convert the metric to English measurement.

REFLECTIONS: Return to the original chart showing what the students did not know. Ask:

1. What have you learned . . . ?

2. Why do you think this is important?

3. How were your teammates helpful?

· · · · · · · · · · · · · · ·   **THE RUBRIC: MEASUREMENT MAGIC**   · · · · · · · · · · · · ·

Standard: Makes accurate conversions between two distance measurement systems.

Criterion	1	2	3	4
Distance	60% or over	70% or over	80% or over	90% or over

Tools: Multiple-choice test

Comments:

_____

_____

_____

Scale	
_____	= A
_____	= B
_____	= C
Below ___	= Not Yet

Final Grade: _____

Make Your Own

LESSON TITLE: _____

TARGETED INTELLIGENCE: _Logical/Mathematical_ _____

SUPPORTING INTELLIGENCES: _____

THINKING SKILLS: _____

SOCIAL SKILLS: _____

CONTENT FOCUS: _____

MATERIALS: _____

TASK FOCUS: _____

PRODUCTS: _____

PROBLEM: _____

ACTIVITY: _____

_____

_____

_____

_____

_____

_____

_____

_____

_____

_____

_____

REFLECTIONS: _____

_____

_____

THE RUBRIC

Standard:

Criteria	1	2	3	4

Tools:

Comments:

_____

_____

_____

Final Grade: _____

Scale

_____ = A

_____ = B

_____ = C

Below ___ = Not Yet

Reflection

Reflections on my assessment of logical/mathematical performances:

What worked well in my classroom? _____

_____

_____

What would I like to change in my lesson and/or assessment of the lesson? _____

_____

_____

What help do I need in improving this assessment? _____

_____

_____

What are other ideas I want to try for assessing this intelligence? _____

_____

_____

Notes: _____

_____

_____

Ideas I most want to use:_____

_____

_____

_____

_____

_____

Assessing Performances in Visual/Spatial Intelligence

What is visual/spatial intelligence?

Visual/spatial intelligence is the capacity to perceive the visual world accurately and to be able to re-create one's visual experiences. It involves the ability to see form, color, shape, and texture in the "mind's eye" and to transfer these to concrete representation in art forms.

This intelligence begins with sharpening of the sensorimotor perceptions of the world around us. The eye discriminates color, shape, form, texture, spatial depth, dimensions, and relationships. As the intelligence develops, eye-hand coordination and small muscle control enable the individual to reproduce the perceived shapes and colors in a variety of media. The painter, sculptor, architect, gardener, cartographer, drafter, graphic designer, and house painter all transfer the images in their minds to the new object they are making or improving. In this way, visual perceptions are mixed with prior knowledge and experience, emotions, and images to create a new vision for others to experience.

Why is visual/spatial intelligence important in the curriculum?

On the aesthetic side, development of the visual/spatial intelligence creates the climate that gives birth to the painters, sculptors, and photographers who record our cultural history in images rather than words. If a picture is truly worth a thousand words, then visual artists are a culture's most valuable communicators.

For the many who don't become successful artists, the appreciation of perspective, color, shape, and form enriches the experience of viewing fine art in a museum or browsing a new car showroom. Beyond the nurturing of future artists, attention to this intelligence has practical value. Instruction in design principles and practices, spatial reasoning, and hand-eye coordination lays the foundation for careers in graphic design, architecture, film and video production, fashion design, advertising and marketing, computer design in a multitude of fields, cartooning, and cartography. For those who don't pursue a formal career in the visual arts, the visual/spatial intelligence developed in school can help them make more aesthetic decisions concerning their homes and wardrobes; help them become better drivers; or help them in choosing a hobby in ceramics, calligraphy, computer graphics, or gardening. In the classroom, development of visual/spatial skills assists with spatial reasoning in geometric forms, development of depth and angle perception for interpreting graphs and charts, and the production of class projects with visual appeal.

What classroom practices develop visual/spatial intelligence?

In a multiage classroom, primary students work at building a diorama of ancient Egypt. Using soap, they carve to scale sculptures of the famous architectural monuments: the obelisk, the pyramid, and the Sphinx. With the help of handheld calculators, weighted strings, crayons, and chart paper, they start with sketches of each monument. Next they measure a scaled map to determine placement of each monument. Finally, they carve the sculptures and place them in their floor map of the scene. After giving the initial instructions and the materials to each group, the teacher moves among the groups to check for understanding, to coach, and to ask individuals to explain what they are doing. After all the maps and monuments are done, the class takes a walking tour from table to table to note the different ways each group created its diorama.

In a middle grade classroom, student groups work over pieces of newsprint. After completing a reading of Frost's "Stopping by Woods on a Snowy Evening," the groups create a sequenced cartoon strip. The completed strip tells the story as if it occurred in the students' neighborhood. The students are challenged by the teacher to create a new ending, dialogue balloons, and local characters. On the board, the teacher lists the criteria and the indicators for a high-quality cartoon. On the overhead, samples of two popular cartoon strips remind the students of what might be good and bad examples.

In a secondary English classroom, groups of three work with newsprint, markers, their notebooks, and the text for Hawthorne's *The Scarlet Letter*. Following the teacher's precise instructions, each group sketches a Venn diagram.

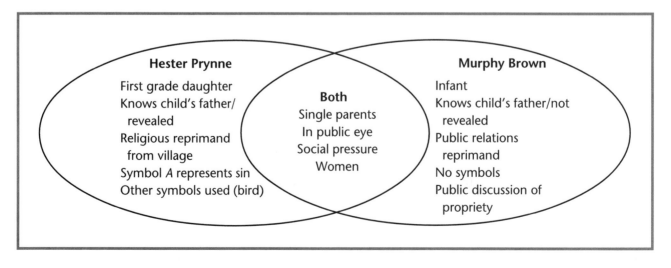

The visual format enables the students to organize their thoughts as they compare and contrast the two characters. When the Venns are done, each group creates a poster ad that portrays the key similarities and differences. Although this project is essentially literary (the verbal/linguistic intelligence), the teacher outlines a visual rubric as well as a verbal/linguistic rubric for judging the final products.

What standards could a teacher use to develop a rubric for visual/spatial intelligence?

Spatial reasoning

Spatial reasoning is the ability to determine why and how visual elements connect in proportion. Like logical reasoning, it is based on "if . . . then" statements. "If this color matches with this color, then. . . ." If I draw this shape at this size, then the next shape must be ____ size to be in proportion."

Spatial reasoning is the foundation standard for this intelligence. First, it is the easiest to measure. Second, it has the greatest transferability. Third, it is essential to all the disciplines that require visual renderings.

Spatial relationship

The spatial relationship standard is a guide for determining how well a student can see the connections among colors, forms, textures, and shapes. Because of the holistic nature of seeing visual relationships, there is a special danger when delineating the criteria of success for this standard. The tendency is to create criteria and indicators that separate the parts into discrete segments. While separation may assist in the instructional phase for emphasis, this standard should highlight criteria that help students connect parts to the whole. For instance, a standard that guides how students perceive the various visual factors, such as color and shape, might read, "The student will identify and explain how the artist's use of color enhances the completed work." A less helpful standard would read, "The student will distinguish between color and shape." Thus, a criterion for this standard would encourage the teacher to note high performance in a secondary art class as "The student will explain valid reasons for his or her color selection as that selection enhances the tone of the finished work." In the primary grades, the criterion for high performance might read, "The student water-colored a neighborhood scene so that the color communicates the mood desired."

Flexibility

The flexibility standard in this intelligence speaks to students' ability to appreciate and/or make a visual representation from multiple perspectives. A notable example of a flexible artist is the French impressionist, Claude Monet. In his series on the "Cathedral of Charles" or the famous

"Water Lily" series, Monet was able to show the same scene with a variety of light effects. He was not locked into one way of painting the scenes.

To develop flexibility in students' visual/spatial intelligence, the teacher can establish a simple numerical standard against which a variety of assignments can be measured. For instance, the standard might call for the student's final art portfolio to include work in at least three art media. A different standard might call for the student to demonstrate flexibility in his or her single-subject rendering painted to achieve three different tones of feeling.

Originality

Originality is one of the most difficult standards to measure. It is also one of the most telling. Is the completed work one that has never been painted or sculpted in the history of art? Or is it a rendering that is a first-time success for this student? What are the qualities that make it original?

Questions such as these make it even more important to delineate the standard and the criteria for developing students' visual talent. The standard of "the first time in history" would be unrealistic and unfair for a classroom. While it is wonderful for a teacher to uncover a budding talent who has original insights, it is more practical that he or she set the standard in relation to the individual's development. Thus, the appropriate standard would encourage students to take a different approach than they've tried before. "Students demonstrate in their completed work that they are able to select an approach that is different from what they or their classmates have previously attempted." A high performance criterion for a primary student might read: "Demonstrates the ability to select a new and wider range of colors for art work." In a secondary photography class, the high performance standard might indicate how the student demonstrates in each new photo series a use of light he or she has not previously attempted.

Persistence

Persistence is a standard that has special value in this intelligence. Stories of starving artists who worked for years to perfect their craft are without end. For several decades, the impressionists had to wait out derision and scorn from the established art world. Georgia O'Keeffe had to overcome the obstacles that blocked a talented female's entrance into the art establishment. Today, her work stands as a tribute to her talent and persistence.

A persistence standard permits quantitative measurement more readily than some of the other standards for this intelligence. For instance, the standard can call for observations of the number of times a student starts and restarts a ceramic bowl that keeps shattering.

A high performance criterion would describe the student's willingness to restart a project each time the technique fails. In a less quantitative tone, the criterion might simply note that the student never complains when a project fails.

What is a sample rubric for visual/spatial intelligence?

Today's children have more opportunity to develop their visual/spatial intelligence than any other generation in history. After thousands of hours of TV, electronic games, and a saturation of visual magazines, they may respond more easily to the picture than they respond to the printed word. The classroom affords many opportunities to capitalize on their visual/spatial awareness. In addition to heightening students' appreciation of the visual and graphic arts, it is easy for today's teacher to design lessons and assessments that integrate visual designs with the academic curriculum. In this way, students advance several intelligences at one time.

THE RUBRIC: MULTIPLE POINTS OF VIEW

Standard: Sketches inanimate object from three points of view, using different lighting and different coloring for each point of view.

Criteria	1	2	3	4
Color Variation	one point of view	two points of view with color change	three points of view with color change	three points of view with subtle color change
Different Lighting	single light source	light source differs in two sketches	light sources differ in each sketch	distinct light source and shadows in each sketch
Side View	single side view	two side views differ	three side views differ slightly	three side views differ significantly
Background	single background	two different backgrounds	three different backgrounds	three different backgrounds well balanced

Tools: PMI; group observation check list

Comments:

_____

_____

_____

Scale	
_____	= A
_____	= B
_____	= C
Below ___	= Not Yet

Final Grade: _____

What assessment tools are most useful for the visual/spatial intelligence?

Product portfolios

One of the oldest methods artists have used to show their works to prospective clients is the portfolio. The portfolio comprises finished pieces that the artist thinks might attract a buyer. In art schools, the portfolio is also a way for the student to gather examples of his or her best work as he or she prepares to graduate. A committee reviews the portfolio and judges whether the student deserves a diploma. (Ted Sizer [1984] advocated this approach for his Essential Schools.)

The portfolio is an easy way to collect student work in the visual/spatial intelligence. The student can use the rubric as a guideline for choosing the visual works he or she wants to include. He or she can also use the rubric as a cue for completing a check list or a written evaluation explaining those choices. Evaluation of the entire portfolio against the standards is done each quarter or semester.

Processfolios

Howard Gardner expresses concern about the overemphasis on product evaluation in American schools. He prefers the evaluation of the process. For the visual/spatial intelligence, the teacher provides check lists or written summaries of work in progress. The student includes these in the folio. At key times in the year, the teacher and the student review these process evaluations and prepare a final evaluation measured against the criteria.

Projects

Team projects work very well with this intelligence. Projects may include dioramas, group-made sculptures, videos, slide shows and films, period costume making, wall murals of historic or literary events, or the creation of historic artifacts. Assessment with check lists, scales, student written and oral self-evaluations as well as teacher written or tape-recorded evaluations referenced to a visual/spatial standard provide a number of assessment options.

Exhibitions

Exhibitions range from primary "show and tell" to presentations of a Ph.D. defense. In an exhibition, the student or a collaborative group presents evidence of its work to a reviewer. The reviewer, using a standard-based assessment tool, assesses the worth of the presentation. In this intelligence, common exhibitions include art shows, video previews, the use of charts and graphs, and poster presentations of materials drawn from other disciplines, such as math, science, or social studies.

Logs and journals

One of the most famous journals in history was the diary of Leonardo da Vinci. In his diaries he not only recorded his thoughts, he included mathematical calculations and many, many sketches and drawings. He noted his many successes, but more regularly assessed the worth of his own ideas and works. Thus, his diary was a valuable record of his work and the thoughts that prompted his flood of inventions.

A simple format for a journal entry is the "What? So What? Now What?" set of reflective questions (Fogarty and Bellanca, 1989, p. 235). In response to the first question, the student sketches his or her idea. To answer the second question, he or she sketches applications or variations of the idea. For the third, he or she records the steps needed to finish out the idea.

Taped feedback

As a teacher monitors the creative visuals that students are making, reflective feedback is a very helpful tool. While teachers usually write down feedback and give each student a sheet of paper with comments, teachers can use just as easily a tape recorder. With a separate tape labeled for each student, the teacher reviews a completed work and makes comments. While the most important comments focus on the standards and criteria, it is not unusual for the teacher to make comments about special features of the work that require corrective action or are especially noteworthy.

How do I align assessment with a lesson focusing on visual/spatial intelligence?

The following are sample lessons and assessments that focus on visual/spatial intelligence.

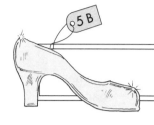

Sample Lesson: Visual/Spatial

Trend Collage

TARGETED INTELLIGENCE: Visual/Spatial

SUPPORTING INTELLIGENCES: Verbal/Linguistic, Interpersonal, Logical/Mathematical

THINKING SKILLS: Trend analysis, decision making, gathering evidence, visualizing

SOCIAL SKILLS: Listening, ownership, and accountability

CONTENT FOCUS: Social studies

MATERIALS: Magazines, newspapers, student logs or journals, glue, scissors, posterboard

TASK FOCUS: Generalizing and analyzing trends

PRODUCT: A collage showing a trend

PROBLEM: How to prove a "generalization" with data

ACTIVITY:

1. Assign the students to groups of three. Instruct each group to select one of the following topics: vacations, cars, colors, car sizes, car styles, highways, careers, movies, books, advertisements, recreation, schools, home electronics, families, politics, health, food, sports.

2. For one week, each group will scan newspapers, magazines, and other available materials in print (i.e., brochures from a car agency), gathering at least 25 samples or items related to its selected topic. If students analyze the samples and make at least one accurate generalization about a trend they see in relation to the topic, they will succeed in the task of proving a generalization with data or evidence. For instance, if the group selects "highways" and students find 25 pictures or articles describing the decay of the interstate highway system and no more than five samples depict the system expanding or improving, students will have sufficient data to generalize and determine a trend (the data having a 80-20 ratio, which would support the generalization). If students find more than 25 samples, they should maintain the 80-20 ratio to adequately support the generalization and determine a trend.

3. After students have gathered sufficient data to prove a generalization (having enough samples to indicate a trend), each group is to construct a collage with selected items that support the generalization the group is making.

4. If students cannot identify a trend in the data/samples they have gathered on the topic by using the 80-20 ratio or rule of generalization, they may substitute some "trend indicators." For instance, a possible trend would be indicated by at least 40% of the samples falling within a certain category.

5. As students finish the trend collages, ask each student to respond to the following:
   a. What is the trend that your group identified?
   b. Explain your evidence.
   c. How strong is your evidence for the generalization you made?

6. Discuss with the class the following questions:
   a. What are the meanings of the terms "generalization" and "trend"?
   b. What are some instances (outside of the class) in which you might use the 80-20 rule of generalization to determine a trend?
   c. How is thinking about generalizations different from brainstorming? from drawing conclusions? from making analogies?

7. Have students complete one of the following sentences in their logs:

A generalization is like _____ because . . .

A trend is like _____ because . . .

When I make generalizations, I need to remember . . .

A trend I would like to reverse is _____ because . . .

THE RUBRIC: TREND COLLAGE

Standard: Creates a collage with evidence of proof for a generalization.

Criteria	1	2	3	4
Trend Identified	fad—other than trend—identified	trend not of consequence	consequential trend	consequential with universal impact
Sufficient and Necessary Data	weak data	sufficient or necessary data	sufficient and necessary data	overpowering data
Collage Reflects Generalization	random sampling	two to three connections	four to six connections	seven or more connections
Collage Has Visual Appeal	elements have no relationships	obvious or superficial connections	significant connections	unified vision

Tools: What? So What? Now What?; peer observation chart; check list

Comments:

_____

_____

_____

Scale	
_____	= A
_____	= B
_____	= C
Below ___	= Not Yet

Final Grade: _____

Sample Lesson: Visual/Spatial

Learning Assessment Album

TARGETED INTELLIGENCE: Visual/Spatial

SUPPORTING INTELLIGENCES: Verbal/Linguistic, Intrapersonal, Interpersonal

THINKING SKILLS: Interpretation, prediction, analysis

SOCIAL SKILLS: Respecting others, active listening

CONTENT FOCUS: Study skills, photography skills (if a camera is available for use during class)

MATERIALS: Photographs, newspapers/magazines, drawing materials, photo albums

TASK FOCUS: Students develop assessment skills.

PRODUCT: Album of visual artifacts (including but not limited to photographs) related to learning unit

PROBLEM: How to assess major learnings during a 4- to 8-week class unit by using a visual format

ACTIVITY:

1. Divide the class into small groups at the beginning of the unit or lesson.

2. Assign specific days or weeks of the unit to each group. Over the following weeks, have student groups analyze what their learnings are for their assigned times. Have members of the group review the following rubric before they begin work on the album.

3. Have group members collect visual/print artifacts for their time period that reflect their learnings at the time. These items may be photographs as well as visual artifacts (pictures or other illustrative matter) from newspapers and/or magazines. Students may take photographs or draw their own illustrations in relation to the learning process during their assigned times.

4. Instruct the group members to select the artifacts that are of the best quality and accurately represent their learnings to be included in an album that is organized chronologically—covering the time period of the unit. (This project can be done by compiling one class album or by having each group compile a separate album.) The album should include an index listing the days/weeks of the learning unit and the corresponding visual artifacts.

5. Have each group provide a written explanation, a summary of their contributions to the learning assessment album.

THE RUBRIC: LEARNING ASSESSMENT ALBUM

Standard: Shows self-assessment by compiling a group album.

Criteria	1	2	3	4
Album Is Complete	two or more missing sets of visual artifacts	one set missing	one set of visual artifacts per day assigned	varied visual artifacts for days assigned
Selected Visual Artifacts Reflect Learnings	no clear connection to learnings	one picture per concept connects	two to three pictures demonstrate each concept	multiple pictures, multiple concepts
Album Is Organized	random organization	some material in sequence	sequential organization throughout	sequential organization; index included
Quality of Photos Selected	photos in album do not reflect learnings	some photos not appropriate, many out of focus	appropriate photos, most in focus	appropriate photos, all in focus
Explanations for Contributions Are Complete	no significant explanations for artifacts	one explanation per page	basic explanation provided for each artifact	in-depth explanation for each artifact

Tools: Observation chart; journals; PMI

Comments:

_____

_____

_____

Scale	
_____	= A
_____	= B
_____	= C
Below ____	= Not Yet

Final Grade: _____

How can I assess visual/spatial intelligence when it is integrated across the curriculum?

Visual/spatial intelligence is one of the most easily integrated intelligences. Teaching strategies that develop the other intelligences can extend and support multidisciplinary learning on a visual/spatial base. The reverse is also true—visual/spatial strategies can be woven into projects and activities from other intelligences. Finally, project-based learning makes an excellent vehicle for integrating the visual/spatial intelligence with the other intelligences.

To build on a visual/spatial base, primary students learn to make a collage. The evaluation is built on a rubric that assesses how well they complete the collage project. To enrich the collage, the teacher instructs the students to apply some of the measurement skills learned in math (logical/mathematical) and to research an author they are studying in language arts (verbal/linguistic). The teacher has the option of integrating the rubric with multiple standards.

It is also possible to reverse the base. For instance, the teacher may want to enrich the creation of a "big book" by having students also draw the pictures for the story. In a secondary social studies class, the teacher could require the students to add charts and graphs to a sociology report. In both cases, he or she may elect to use a rubric for the targeted intelligence or for the combined intelligences.

The teacher may design a project rubric to assess several intelligences that are developed. For instance, the teacher might use Fogarty's shared model (1991) to design the science-language

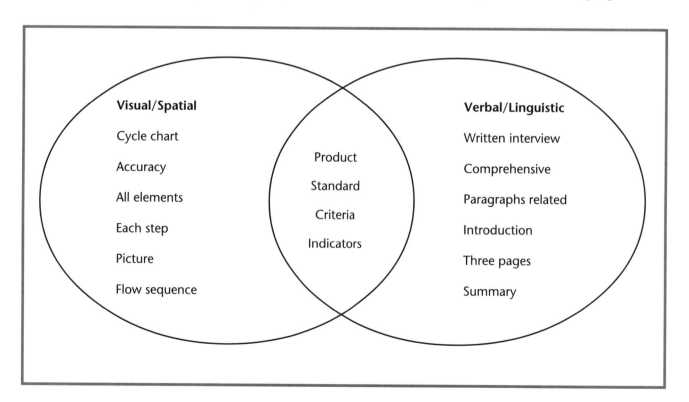

arts lesson on photosynthesis. The final products, developed collaboratively in small groups, would include a chart depicting the cycle of photosynthesis and a typed interview with a local florist or park department botanist. The shared model, represented by a Venn diagram, makes a helpful tool for designing the rubric to focus on the visual/spatial and verbal/linguistic intelligences.

The webbed model (Fogarty, 1991) also lends itself to project assessment. For instance, if the targeted intelligence is visual/spatial, the learning project can be the creation of a mobile. Using the webbed model, the teacher can integrate interpersonal (cooperative groups), intrapersonal (log entry), musical (research a composer), and verbal/linguistic (oral presentation) intelligences into the project's creation. To assess the project, the teacher could use a similar web to create the rubric. He or she would integrate standards for the visual (flexibility), interpersonal (trust), intrapersonal (accuracy), musical (understanding), and verbal/linguistic (comprehension).

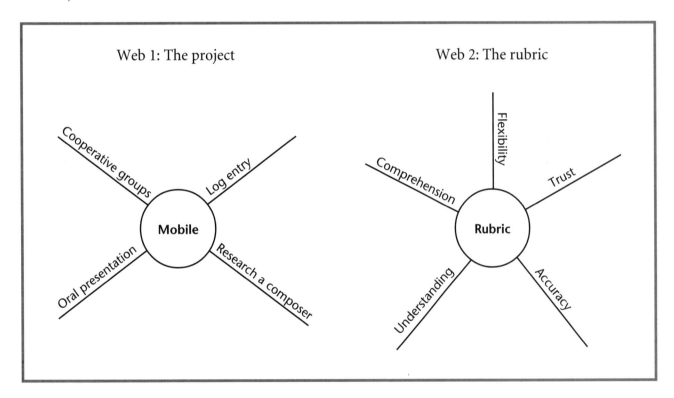

PRIMARY EXAMPLE

Sample Lesson: Visual/Spatial

Shape Link

TARGETED INTELLIGENCE: Visual/Spatial

SUPPORTING INTELLIGENCES: Verbal/Linguistic, Intrapersonal, Logical/Mathematical

THINKING SKILLS: Predicting, analyzing

SOCIAL SKILLS: Respect for others, accepting responsibility

CONTENT FOCUS: Geometric shapes

MATERIALS: Envelope of 15 to 20 geometric shapes of various sizes and colors cut from construction paper and a work surface

TASK FOCUS: Student teams develop a shared picture from the shapes.

PRODUCT: Picture creation

PROBLEM: How to make the geometric shapes form a creative design.

ACTIVITY:

1. Assign partners. Name one an A and the other a B.
2. Give an envelope of geometric shapes to each team (triangles, squares, circles, rectangles).
3. A chooses a shape and places it on the work surface.
4. B chooses a shape and connects it to A's shape.
5. This continues through several sequences of A then B until both agree that their picture is complete.
6. Continue the game by making more pictures.
7. Have students reflect on these questions in their journals:
    a. What did we learn about sharing?
    b. How did we share?
    c. What is another picture we could form from these same shapes?
    d. What did you discover about the linking of the shapes?

THE RUBRIC: SHAPE LINK

Standard: Uses geometric shapes in a cooperative design project.

Criteria	1	2	3	4
Patterns	makes random connections	duplicates patterns; exact productions	replicates patterns; models	makes unique patterns
Rationale , Explanation (Journal Writings)	describes minimal learning	describes necessary, sufficient connections	describes strong, necessary, and sufficient links	also gives examples of other uses of these patterns
Shapes	uses one or two shapes	uses three or four different shapes	uses five or six different shapes	uses seven or eight different shapes

Tools: Plus/Minus cards; check list

Comments:

_____

_____

_____

Final Grade: _____

Scale	
_____	= A
_____	= B
_____	= C
Below ____	= Not Yet

Make Your Own

TITLE : _____

TARGETED INTELLIGENCE: *Visual/Spatial* _____

SUPPORTING INTELLIGENCES: _____

THINKING SKILLS: _____

SOCIAL SKILLS: _____

CONTENT FOCUS: _____

MATERIALS: _____

TASK FOCUS: _____

PRODUCT: _____

PROBLEM: _____

ACTIVITY _____

_____

_____

_____

_____

_____

_____

_____

_____

_____

_____

_____

_____

_____

REFLECTIONS: _____

_____

THE RUBRIC

Standard:

Criteria	1	2	3	4

Tools:

Comments:

_____

_____

_____

Final Grade: _____

Scale

_____ = A

_____ = B

_____ = C

Below ___ = Not Yet

Reflection

Reflections on my assessment of visual/spatial performances:

What worked well in my classroom? _____

_____

_____

What would I like to change in my lesson and/or assessment of the lesson? _____

_____

_____

What help do I need in improving this assessment? _____

_____

_____

What are other ideas I want to try for assessing this intelligence? _____

_____

_____

Notes: _____

_____

_____

Ideas I most want to use:_____

_____

_____

_____

_____

_____

Assessing Performances in Bodily/Kinesthetic Intelligence

What is bodily/kinesthetic intelligence?

Bodily/kinesthetic intelligence enables us to control and interpret body motions, manipulate physical objects, and establish harmony between the mind and the body. The Spartans of ancient Greece built their culture around the importance of the body, its looks, and its performance. In modern times, the Olympics carries on that tradition.

It is mistake, however, to think that the development of this intelligence is limited to athletics. Imagine a surgeon without the fine small-motor control to perform an intricate heart operation or a plane navigator who cannot fine-tune his instruments. How would you like a porch built by a carpenter who can't hit the head on a nail? Would you hire a plumber who can't straighten pipes with a wrench?

Marcel Marceau is an example of an individual with a highly developed bodily/kinesthetic intelligence. With his body, the mime can create many different personalities: the bully, the recluse, and the clown. He can suggest the mountain climber, the butterfly, waves cresting, or the concepts of good and evil or freedom and bondage with equal facility. More amazingly, he can create a number of these illusions simultaneously.

Why is bodily/kinesthetic intelligence important in the curriculum?

In a high-tech, consumptive world, the "couch potato" disease afflicts students even before they start school. Wealth or poverty seems to make little difference. The statistics on passive TV watching and snack food munching made clear why today's young people need multiple avenues for developing healthy lifestyles.

Within the traditional curriculum, health and physical education have been considered frills for the many or extracurricular activity for the elite athlete. But now as our society begins to understand the cost of poor health attitudes and habits, the need to integrate health programs across the curriculum for all students is becoming apparent.

Good health care is less costly than poor health repair. In schools, the traditional model of leaving the full responsibility to the P.E. and sports departments for developing the bodily/kinesthetic intelligence is not enough. In a world where longevity is increasing, it is important that lifestyle habits be formed at an early age. These habits, built on the beliefs that healthy bodies make healthy minds, that people who develop early habits of positive health continue these habits through life, and that such habits are essential for a low-risk lifestyle in the senior years, encourage young students to develop active, physical lives that are built on the principles of whole health. In this context, every child becomes an athlete, not a superstar, who develops bodily/kinesthetic talents, habits, and attitudes for a lifetime of good health.

The development of the bodily/kinesthetic intelligence also has instructional significance. When teachers use concrete manipulatives to introduce new concepts, they put into practice a basic constructivist principle: They create the concrete sensations that Piaget pointed out were so necessary for the student to form a concept. When teachers start with abstract ideas for which students have no prior knowledge, it is very difficult for students to form the abstraction. Techniques that put this theory into practice draw upon and develop the bodily/kinesthetic intelligence.

Students develop their bodily/kinesthetic intelligence when they are actively involved in physical performances. Intramural sports programs which allow all students to practice new skills and learn new games are an important start. Role playing and mime go a step beyond in having students simulate a character in history or literature or act out in concrete terms an abstract scientific principle, such as photosynthesis or the transfer of energy. When used in this way, the bodily/kinesthetic intelligence enriches conceptualization and solidifies memory.

What classroom practices develop bodily/kinesthetic intelligence?

In the primary grades, the structured lab or structured center time is an opportunity to engage children through the bodily/kinesthetic intelligence. For example, the teacher may set up center activities that engage small and gross motor skills as the students use manipulative blocks to problem solve. The children receive several colored blocks and must connect them in specified patterns.

In addition to the center approach, primary teachers may ask students to use physical movement to explain an idea. For instance, after hearing the teacher read a story, the students form groups of three to five to dance and mime their interpretations of the story. In other instances, they can use their bodies to act out scientific principles, such as the difference between being an animal and a vegetable or between a solid and a liquid.

Use of manipulatives need not be limited to the lower grades. In Richmond, Virginia, a master teacher of talented students uses manipulatives to introduce each math concept in geometry. For instance, in her lesson introducing circumference, the class starts with the hands-on measurement of various drinking glasses and cups. Next, the class uses paper plates, tape measures, and string to test hypotheses and develop abstract rules about radius and circumference. Finally, they transfer what they learned with the hands-on materials to abstract algorithms.

The use of creative dramatics allows students of all ages to engage in active performances. In creative dramatics, kinesthetic performances engage students in learning how to feel the roles, the setting, the problem, or the story line and turn the feelings into a dramatic presentation. In a middle school in Indiana, students write and perform their autobiographies, biographies of famous historic figures, and characterizations of major figures from novels and short stories. In Lawton, Oklahoma, primary and middle grade teachers use the STARS substance prevention program. This program starts with the youngest children learning positive health and nutrition habits as the foundation of prevention. The children engage in active tasks which require them to role-play the positive effects of healthy decisions.

What standards could a teacher use to develop a rubric for bodily/kinesthetic intelligence?

Creativity and originality

In creating problems to solve with bodily/kinesthetic intelligence, novel performances are an effective instructional tool. Originality evolves when students physically display an idea which at first glance has nothing to do with this intelligence.

Consistency

Students in a Delaware middle school who watched the 1994 Olympics noted how important consistency was in the medal winners' success. In their discussions they talked about the champion bobsledders who made four runs and never touched a side. One student observed how the best skaters landed their jumps over and over. These students show through their examples that consistency means the ability to perform a task uniformly every time.

Perseverance

This intelligence usually involves a student-centered, "hands-on" experience. Does the student stay on task? Does the student give up easily when the going gets difficult? If one way doesn't work, does he or she try another way or instantly seek help? For example, consider learning how to shoot a basketball. Some students have highly developed motor skills; the layup is very easy for them. Now, move the student away from the basket to the foul line. This is a tougher challenge. It requires practice. It also requires perseverance. How long will the student practice to raise his or her average to 70 percent or higher even when the ball never seems to sink?

Flexibility

In the bodily/kinesthetic intelligence, flexibility is a major standard, requiring teachers and students to assess the different approaches that might be taken to perform a skill or do a task. For instance, how many different ways might a skater interpret music during a free-skate exhibition? How many different approaches might a soccer player take in defending against an opponent? How many interpretations are there for expressing a character's personality? How many approaches are there to solving a math problem with manipulatives?

What is a sample rubric for the bodily/kinesthetic intelligence?

For many American middle and high schools, sound performance in this intelligence is relegated to interscholastic, athletic programs. In many elementary school no performance in this intelligence is possible. At both extremes, bodily/kinesthetic performances are considered useful only outside the classroom. This need not be so. In fact, it is our contention that development of

THE RUBRIC: BASKETBALL

Standard: Defends against a three-point shot using a demonstrated strategy.

Criterion	1	2	3	4
Defends Against a Three-Point Shot	rarely demonstrates the strategy during a game	uses the strategy during a game	demonstrates three modifications of the strategy during a game	demonstrates three or more modifications of the strategy and prevents the opponent from scoring

Tools: Check list
Comments:

_____

_____

_____

Final Grade: _____

Scale	
_____	= A
_____	= B
_____	= C
Below ___	= Not Yet

this intelligence is not only beneficial for all students, it is also important in every classroom. If nothing else is possible, bodily/kinesthetic activities can enhance motivation and success across the curriculum. Rubrics that guide development of this intelligence and enhance motivation in the classroom as well as in the gym are easy to design. Consider the basketball rubric on page 144.

What assessment tools are most useful for bodily/ kinesthetic intelligence?

PMI

An especially helpful tool in assessing this intelligence is de Bono's (1983) PMI chart, which may be configured in several ways.

P (+)	Strengths	or	**P**	Things you did well
M (-)	Weaknesses	or	**M**	Ways to improve
I (?)	Questions, concerns	or	**I**	Interesting comments

After the student completes a performance, he or she completes the PMI. Afterwards, the teacher adds elements that were missed.

TEAM RELAY		
P	**M**	**I**
Pluses	*Minuses*	*Interesting comments*
Practiced baton hand-off	Almost missed third hand-off	More practice needed
Encouraged each other	Got mad at Sammy for miss	Encourage more
Won the race		Felt great
(t) *Improved time*	(t) *Spacing for hand-off*	(t) *Count out loud*

Comfort-discomfort continuum

When students can show what they know, explain the process step by step, and express how they feel about their learning comfort level, they effectively demonstrate their understanding. Taking all of this into account, teachers can reteach what is needed to be retaught, move on to the next step, or give more of the same. They are able to do this accurately because they are getting enough data and asking for the correct information.

PRIMARY EXAMPLE

Making patterns with blocks

|-----------------------------|-----------------------------|-----------------------------|-----------------------------|

comfort   discomfort

MIDDLE SCHOOL EXAMPLE

Mime an animal's actions and appearance and have peers guess what the animal is.

|-----------------------------|-----------------------------|-----------------------------|-----------------------------|

comfort   discomfort

explanation

SECONDARY EXAMPLE

Teach new vocabulary words to a peer by acting out the meanings

|-----------------------------|-----------------------------|-----------------------------|-----------------------------|

comfort   discomfort

explanation

Journal entry

After a physical activity has been completed, appropriate journal entries are

> Today I learned. . . .
>
> Today I was surprised. . . .
>
> What I found most difficult to do in this activity was. . . .
>
> What I found easiest to do in this activity was. . . .
>
> It is important that I improve. . . .

Observation check lists

Active performances lend themselves well to observation check lists. If a school has a video camera and recorder, student groups can record each other "doing" a physical activity. Afterwards, the teacher, a parent, or the students can use a check list to assess the quality of the performance.

PRIMARY EXAMPLE

Tying Shoelaces

1. _____
2. _____
3. _____
4. _____

MIDDLE SCHOOL EXAMPLE

Taking Notes

1. _____
2. _____
3. _____
4. _____

SECONDARY EXAMPLE

Historic Drama

1. ____ Historically accurate costumes
2. ____ Feeling tone in speaking role
3. ____ Clear articulation
4. ____ Gestures fit the words
5. ____ Other _____

How do I align assessment with a lesson focusing on bodily/kinesthetic intelligence?

The following is an activity that focuses on bodily/kinesthetic intelligence, having students work on eye-hand coordination and game-playing skills.

Sample Lesson: Bodily/Kinesthetic

Rock, Paper, Scissors

TARGETED INTELLIGENCE: Bodily/Kinesthetic

SUPPORTING INTELLIGENCES: Verbal/Linguistic, Interpersonal, Visual/Spatial

THINKING SKILL: Synthesis

SOCIAL SKILLS: Game-playing skills, friendly competition (being a good sport)

CONTENT FOCUS: Eye-hand coordination, following directions

MATERIALS: None

TASK FOCUS: Students develop coordination skills by playing a friendly game.

PRODUCT: None

PROBLEM: To play "rock, paper, scissors" by the rules

ACTIVITY:

1. Check to see who in the class has previously played the game (rock, paper, scissors). Explain the following game rules and have two volunteers demonstrate the actions of the game—which is played in pairs.
   a. A fist = rock; two fingers (index and middle) = scissors; a hand, palm down = paper.
   b. Paper wraps rock; scissors cuts paper; rock breaks scissors.

   On the count of three, each person sticks out either a fist, two fingers, or a hand (palm down), the choice being up to each of the two players. For example, the person who sticks out two fingers will lose to the person who sticks out a fist (rock breaks scissors).

2. Allow students to form two-person teams and play the game. Hold elimination rounds until there is a final winner.

THE RUBRIC: GAME-PLAYING

Standard: Demonstrates understanding of rock, paper, scissors game rules.

Criteria	1	2	3	4
Follows Rules of Game	does not follow rules	names and follows 50% of the rules	follows rules 75% of the time	follows rules 100% of the time
Speed During Game	last to respond in game	hesitates to respond	often the first to respond	always first to respond
Eye-Hand Coordination During Game	makes many mistakes with hand signals	makes three or four mistakes	makes one or two mistakes	makes no mistakes

Tools: Observation check list

Comments:

_____

_____

_____

Scale	
_____	= A
_____	= B
_____	= C
Below ____	= Not Yet

Final Grade: _____

How can I assess bodily/kinesthetic intelligence when it is integrated across the curriculum?

While health and fitness are increasing in importance in the curriculum, limited school resources and limited time and space in the curriculum make it difficult to include these features in the primary and middle grades. Rather than think about health and fitness as something else to add, a school can integrate health content and fitness activities throughout the day.

1. Use health content (substance abuse prevention, nutrition, body conditioning) as research projects. Make "understanding your health" a major theme for study. Collect a variety of reading materials and other resource documents. Break the theme into subtopics such as nutrition, health care, medicines, and health careers. Have groups of students review the materials and compose lists of questions about the resources. After the students pick the best questions, have them (a) read the material, (b) develop key vocabulary and spelling lists, (c) write summaries, (d) organize the summaries into newspaper or magazine format, (e) create ads for the document, and (f) use a check list or rubric to assess the language arts, fine arts, and thinking skills they have developed.

2. Use kinesthetic activities as learning tools for basic subjects. Biology teacher Robert Kapheim uses mime as the tool for his high school students to learn vocabulary by acting out the meanings of key words. Other teachers use role playing and dance so that students learn about characters and events while expending energy and developing bodily/kinesthetic talents at the same time.

3. Use noncompetitive new games from cultures around the world as part of cross-cultural studies.

4. Design student projects that engage students in manipulation of objects and tools to learn social studies or science concepts. In Elgin, Illinois, teacher teams have their classes construct a mini-Egypt with a ten-foot pyramid, Cleopatra's barge, and other almost life-size artifacts. After costumes are made, the students enact a play they wrote with characters from ancient Egyptian history. Later, other projects include creation of a colonial village with a simulated town meeting, a dramatization of a gold rush conflict, and role plays of famous inventors at the moment of success.

Sample Lesson: Bodily/Kinesthetic

Self-Portrait

TARGETED INTELLIGENCE: Bodily/Kinesthetic

SUPPORTING INTELLIGENCES: Visual/Spatial, Intrapersonal

THINKING SKILL: Assessment

SOCIAL SKILL: Sharing

CONTENT FOCUS: Targeted physical education activity or health lesson

MATERIALS: Journals, magazines, posterboard, glue, scissors

TASK FOCUS: Completing a self-assessment

PRODUCT: A personal collage/self-portrait reflecting a student's performance

PROBLEM: To assess goal completion

ACTIVITY:

1. Provide—or invite each student to bring—the following: scissors, paste, newspapers or old magazines, and a 24" × 36" posterboard for each student.
2. Show some examples of self-assessment by famous athletes, such as published interviews.
3. Show some examples of famous artists' self-portraits. Discuss what each says and how it is said. Share criteria for the self-assessment in the following rubric.
4. Have student pairs review their personal performances and goals for the selected activity or lesson.
5. Invite each student to make a collage focused on one of the units just completed, focusing on self-assessment.
6. Allow twenty to thirty minutes for each student to complete and then sign the collage.
7. Display the collages around the room.
8. Conduct a class discussion on the benefits of a collage as a way to assess personal goals.

THE RUBRIC: SELF-PORTRAIT

Standard: Produces a collage that shows his or her self-assessment of performance goals for

_____.

Criteria	1	2	3	4
Portrait Shows Student's Performance Goal	little connection to goal	some reflection of goal	somewhat elaborated reflection of goal	clear and specific reflection
Portrait Shows Degree of Achievement	achievement weakly shown	concrete example included	original example included	concrete and original examples included
Portrait Shows Personal Involvement	little personal input	some personal input	moderate personal input	high amount of personal input

Tools: Check list, PMI

Comments:

_____

_____

_____

Final Grade: _____

Scale	
_____	= A
_____	= B
_____	= C
Below ___	= Not Yet

Sample Lesson: Bodily/Kinesthetic

Elephant, Kangaroo, Giraffe

TARGETED INTELLIGENCE: Bodily/Kinesthetic

SUPPORTING INTELLIGENCES: None

THINKING SKILL: Analysis

SOCIAL SKILLS: Playing by the rules, teamwork

CONTENT FOCUS: Physical movement, collaboration

MATERIALS: None

TASK FOCUS: Following directions and rules

PRODUCT: None

PROBLEM: How to follow the game rules and repeat movements

ACTIVITY:

1. Stand the students in a large circle shoulder to shoulder.
2. Ask for three volunteers to stand in the center for a demonstration.
3. Have the three volunteers "form" each of three animals using the following directions, reminding the others to watch closely.
   a. Elephant—Have the center student dangle an arm from his or her nose; have the other students frame giant ears from the first student's head.
   b. Kangaroo—Have the center student make a pouch with his or her arms; have the other students bounce up and down.
   c. Giraffe—Have the center student make a long neck with his or her arms and stand on his or her toes; have the others squat down and point to the center student's ankles.
4. After the demonstration, review the guidelines or criteria that will be used for "evaluation" during the game, referring to the following rubric. Then point to three students, other than the volunteers, who are standing side by side. Name one of the three animals. Those students must make that animal as they remember it from the demonstration. Continue the game as you go around the circle, assessing each student's performance as you go.
5. After the game, discuss what was difficult and what was easy about playing "Elephant, Kangaroo, Giraffe."

THE RUBRIC: ELEPHANT, KANGAROO, GIRAFFE

THE RUBRIC: ELEPHANT, KANGAROO, GIRAFFE

Standard: Performs all tasks in conformance with guidelines of game.

Criteria	1	2	3	4
Central Task by Center Student	five or six misses	three or four misses	one or two misses	always performed task; no misses
Side Tasks by Partners on Either Side	five or six misses	three or four misses	one or two misses	always performed task
Combination of Tasks (End Result)	five or six misses	three or four misses	one or two misses	always performed task

Tools: Plus/Minus chart

Comments:

_____

_____

_____

Scale	
_____	= Pass
_____	= Fail

Make Your Own

TITLE: _____

TARGETED INTELLIGENCE: _Bodily/Kinesthetic_____

SUPPORTING INTELLIGENCES: _____

THINKING SKILLS: _____

SOCIAL SKILLS: _____

CONTENT FOCUS: _____

MATERIALS: _____

TASK FOCUS: _____

PRODUCT: _____

PROBLEM: _____

ACTIVITY: _____

_____

_____

_____

_____

_____

_____

_____

_____

_____

_____

_____

_____

REFLECTIONS: _____

_____

_____

================================= **THE RUBRIC** =================================

Standard:

Criteria	1	2	3	4

Tools:

Comments:

_____

_____

_____

Final Grade: _____

Scale
_____ = A
_____ = B
_____ = C
Below ___ = Not Yet

Reflection

Reflections on my assessment of bodily/kinesthetic performances:

What worked well in my classroom? _____

_____

_____

What would I like to change in my lesson and/or assessment of the lesson? _____

_____

_____

What help do I need in improving this assessment? _____

_____

_____

What are other ideas I want to try for assessing this intelligence? _____

_____

_____

Notes: _____

_____

_____

Ideas I most want to use:_____

_____

_____

_____

_____

_____

_____

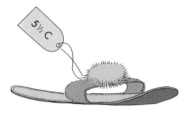

Assessing Performances in Intrapersonal Intelligence

What is intrapersonal intelligence?

Intrapersonal intelligence fosters the ability to know oneself and assume responsibility for one's life and learning. The individual with a strong intrapersonal intelligence is able to understand his or her range of emotions and draw on them to direct his or her behavior. This individual thrives on time to think, to reflect, and to complete self-assessments. The need for such introspection makes this intelligence the most private. In Gardner's words, "the intrapersonal intelligence amounts to little more than the capacity to distinguish a feeling of pleasure from one of pain and, on the basis of such discrimination, to become more involved in or to withdraw from a situation" (1983, p. 239).

This is the intelligence that enables learners to take greater responsibility for their lives and learning. Too few students, Gardner suggests, know that they can take responsibility for their learning, especially when they find themselves in schools that base recognition on external motivations.

This intelligence requires that students have the time to think, reflect, and complete self-assessments that will help them take control and be responsible for their learning choices. The responsible student is most able to access full intellectual potential.

Why is intrapersonal intelligence important in the curriculum?

By helping students develop their intrapersonal intelligence, the classroom teacher moves students out of the factory model of education with its overemphasis on an external locus of control. The teacher encourages the introspective intelligence by moving away from whole-group instruction, lock-step textbook coverage, rigid daily schedules, and rote exercises that have no intrinsic value. Recognizing that the intrapersonal student thrives in a classroom where self-determination is encouraged, the elementary classroom offers many choices in what, when, where, and how to learn. There are several exploratory centers and a quiet corner. Center time is balanced with individual reading time. The opportunities to work in cooperative groups are balanced with time to plan and chart individual learning tasks and to look back at how learning occurred.

The fundamental message that the intrapersonally directed classroom sends is that the students are responsible for their learning. Each student in this kind of classroom is an individual learning project. The teacher is seen as a helper, guide, and support person who makes time for private conversations with students. These conversations help each student analyze his or her strengths and areas needing improvement so that they can make responsible learning choices.

In encouraging this intelligence, both teachers and students have the opportunity to reflect on the relevance of the curriculum. As students become more adept at goal setting, the focus of the curriculum becomes clearer. Students create their own independent assignments and learning becomes more meaningful. Processing information, applying facts in one's own world, realizing weaknesses and strengths, learning to express feelings and be a confident citizen are "traits" teachers can build by providing tasks to challenge the intrapersonal student.

What classroom practices develop intrapersonal intelligence?

Math logs

In a first grade classroom in Arkansas, the teacher begins each math lesson using math logs. This practice was started at the beginning of school. After three months of using math logs two to four days a week, the students are letting her know the thinking steps they follow for solving the problems. They write an example problem and its answer. Afterwards, they write the step-by-step procedure they used to solve the problem. They read and show a peer how they derived the answer.

Stretch-the-mind time

In a multiage elementary classroom in Minnesota, the math problem table at the back of the room has some very high-level tasks to solve. The student goes to the back table and chooses a spot marked off on the table. The problem can stay in that spot and no one else is allowed to use it or play with it.

As the solutions are discovered, students write down their process of solving and the feelings they had as the problem was solved in a "Stretch-the-Mind-Time Journal."

Logs and journals

In a Nebraska middle school exploratory class, students choose a book to read from the shelf in the classroom. As they read, they write in the journal about their reflections, insights, and story plot. Their partners then write back to them with a reaction. Each student is independently responsible for keeping a running list of books read and for reporting the responses in their journals. Those students who were reluctant readers at the beginning of the year are now enjoying the printed word and like to celebrate the joy of reading through their journal reflections. During each grading period students also do reports on the book of their choice. Some do bag reports. They decorate the outside of the bag with illustrations, author, and title. They then put items inside the bag that are appropriate props to tell their classmates about their selection.

To help students at any grade level develop their intrapersonal intelligence, teachers can involve students in goal-setting activities. Teachers can pick a weekly social, personal, or academic goal and ask students to evaluate it. Students begin to make decisions about what personal and academic goals are appropriate for them. They begin to learn how to prioritize their goals and set realistic standards for themselves. Questions they ask themselves include, "What is my goal? Is it achievable? is it believable? Am I capable of achieving this goal?" Students are encouraged to write down their goals so that at the start and end of each week they can review and assess their progress. As the year advances, they add additional goals for themselves.

To help all students develop problem-solving skills, time is spent thinking of "real-world" problems. Students use sequence charts to plan a step-by-step solution to the problem. They are encouraged to come up with alternative solutions and then evaluate which solutions are the most practical or make the most sense. As they practice this decision-making process, they reflect in their double-entry journals. Journal reflections include, "What am I learning?" "How does this problem apply to me?" "How can I use this information?" "How will this solution affect me?" "What are my hopes for this class?" or "What are my hopes for my future?" Students are given many opportunities for journal reflection and look forward to reading the teacher's responses to their thoughts.

Journals are not only useful as a reflective tool; they can also help students process their thinking. At the primary level, journals help students explore their thinking for understanding. At the middle and secondary levels, journals help students analyze for clarity, synthesize into personal meaning, or make critical connections between new information and past experience.

Journal writing can take many forms. It can be a narrative, a quote, a drawing, a cartoon, a diagram, a web, a riddle, a joke, doodles, an opinion, a rebuttal, a dialogue, a flow chart, or an assortment of phrases and ideas. There is no one way to do a journal; it is the doing that is important. The object is to encourage the student to start chronicling his or her thinking, to begin to see how connections are being made, to sense his or her own thought processes. The journal becomes a way for upper-level students to recognize how they think. Do they think systematically or do they make intuitive leaps? Do they make analogies or do they quantify? The journaling process helps students think about their thinking.

Open-ended questions

Teachers can also help students think reflectively in the classroom by asking questions. The questions should be presented with wait-time for serious reflection. The teacher asks a question and then waits at least three to ten seconds so students can think about an appropriate answer.

The teacher does not answer his or her own questions or ask questions that need only a one-word answer. Rather, the questions in the intrapersonal classroom sound like "How would you feel if?. . ." or "What would you do in a similar situation?"

What standards could a teacher use to develop a rubric for intrapersonal intelligence?

Self-awareness

One of the keys to establishing an intrapersonal classroom is the encouragement of self-awareness. One way to do this is to introduce the students to the multiple intelligences. Have them think about the things they like to do. Do they like to draw, sing, dance, play with computers, work in a group, or play sports? The goal is to become aware of which of their intelligences are the strongest.

Reflection

This intelligence is introspective, but reflection is one skill that students can display outwardly. Their reflections can be demonstrated in a variety of ways: in the goals they set for themselves, in the comments they make in their reflective journals, in their self-assessments of their group work, and in the selections they make for their portfolios.

Individual contribution to group goal

As students learn more about themselves, they become aware of their ability to work with others. Because the intrapersonal classroom provides a wide variety of learning situations, there are daily opportunities for small group work as well as working with partners. From these structured activities, students learn the cooperative skills needed for successful group dynamics.

Synthesis

The positive amount of reflective time in the intrapersonal classroom also encourages students to synthesize information. Answering open-ended questions in reflective journals helps students refashion information so they better understand it. Using graphic organizers helps students synthesize information visually.

What is a sample rubric for the intrapersonal intelligence?

The critical standard for intrapersonal intelligence may be "self-awareness." While this may seem to be an outcome (a consequence or result), it is more helpful to see it as a standard. The student who has a great deal of self-awareness is one who has developed a process of "understanding him- or herself." Following Aristotle's dictum, "Know thyself," this person can define the nature of self-awareness and use strategies to increase self-knowledge. Increased self-knowledge leads to a sharpened ability to understand personal strengths and weaknesses and find ways to steer more successfully along the pathways to success. Unlike the infamous Willy Loman in Arthur Miller's *Death of a Salesman*, the student who develops this intelligence according to the standard of self-awareness will indeed know him- or herself.

THE RUBRIC: SELF-AWARENESS

Standard: Assesses progress toward personal achievement of learning goals.

Criteria	1	2	3	4
Number of Goals	one	two	three	four
Daily Reflection on Goals	short entry in log	paragraph with examples	complete assessment tool	assessment tool with ABC criteria
Chart of Progress	shows little gain	shows some gain	shows moderate gain	shows exceedingly high gain
Depth of Reflection	states the means to achieve	+/– assessment of reasons	explains reasons	explains reason with special remarks

Tools: Journals; PMI

Comments:

_____

_____

_____

Scale	
_____	= A
_____	= B
_____	= C
Below ___	= Not Yet

Final Grade: _____

What assessment tools are most useful for intrapersonal intelligence?

Logs and journals

Reflective journals and thinking logs demonstrate a student's self-awareness, capacity for reflection, and/or the ability to analyze or to synthesize. To demonstrate growth, students need to maintain journals over a period of time and chart their own growth patterns.

Because of the reflective nature of this intelligence, reflective journals and thinking logs should be created *by* students *for* student use.

Confidentiality and privacy are very important. The student must control what he or she allows a teacher to read. It isn't necessary for the teacher to read every word in all students' journals. Specific journal entries can be used as the centerpiece of the teacher-student interview, or for peer interviewing. The student can share the "aha" moment in his or her journal that led to self-awareness, or that was compelling, or that became an analytical discussion, or that was a synthesis of two different pieces of information. In the retelling or rereading of that moment, the student's metacognitive understanding is sharpened and he or she more clearly understands how it is that he or she knows. It is as meaningful for the student to share this moment with a peer as with a teacher, because the object is for the student to develop an understanding of his or her ability for learning.

Some adults have serious concerns about student journals. They fear teachers are invading the student's privacy and even his or her family's privacy. Certainly, it is possible for a teacher to misuse the journal in this way. The journal, however, is not a tool in which students are asked to lay bare their private selves. It is a tool in which students can plan and assess their school work and their thinking about how they did their school work. The teacher can review this material to help students develop their cognitive and metacognitive abilities.

Reflections based on a student's "aha" make excellent entries. The aha makes the learner focus on one significant learning during a specified period of time. The teacher can facilitate "aha" entries by stating one of the following at the end of class:

> Today I learned. . . .
> Today I was surprised that. . . .
> Today I realized. . . .

The student writes his or her "aha," puts a box around it, and dates it.

MY AHA

Today I discovered that I am really good at singing. My voice is terrible. I can't keep a tune, but I'm great at rap and my friends like the words I invent.

Aha boxes help the teacher get a quick picture of the student's learning, and the journal helps the teacher know which points the student is learning best.

Another quick entry is using faces for the affective and cognitive domains of feelings. The teacher instructs the students to draw two faces and depict on one their feelings about their comfort during today's class (the affective) and on the other, the way they feel right now with the subject matter they are studying (the cognitive).

If smiley faces are drawn, students do not need to explain.

If some other type of face is drawn, the students let the teacher know why with a quick note.

Another reflective reporting method is the continuum.

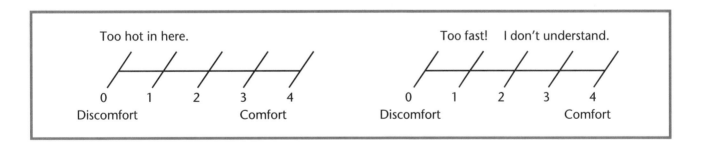

The Interview

The interview is also a strategy to help students assess their personal goal achievements. In reflective discussion, for instance, the student thinks back on several successful group interactions in which he or she demonstrated cooperative group skills. He or she explains his or her contributions to the group task and how those contributions might improve.

Teacher-directed assignments

Carefully constructed teacher-made tests help students demonstrate their ability to analyze and synthesize. The rigor of these thinking skills encourages teachers to present course content so that it "uncovers" ideas rather than "covers" all the facts. By asking students to analyze and synthesize, teachers encourage students to show what they understand. They demonstrate understanding of factual information by restructuring and making supporting connections.

The cultural capsule is an example of a first grade intrapersonal assignment that helps students understand their own heritage and requires the student to analyze how shared artifacts represent their cultural heritage. For this task, each student makes a culture capsule about the culture of his or her family. The capsule includes three items brought from home that represent some aspect of the artistic, cultural, or intellectual accomplishments of the student's heritage. The student may receive help from his or her parents and may share these items with the class. This assignment asks students to make connections to their own heritage in terms of performances, art objects, music, sculpture, handwork, clothing, written documents, or oral stories that were important in their families' lives.

An analysis example for the upper grades is the "Hall of Fame." Students work in groups to brainstorm the major contribution in their own culture or some other culture to civilization. When the list is complete, students choose the contribution they think is most significant. In new groups students select one contribution and brainstorm its major impact. When the brainstorming is over, each student writes individual persuasive essays arguing why this contribution should be included in the "World Civilization Hall of Fame." The final product, the essay, requires students to demonstrate analytical and synthesizing skills.

In each of these evaluation scenarios, students are required to do much more than fill in the work sheet or answer short true or false questions. Students are being asked to evaluate their prior knowledge and apply it in ways that help them understand what is meant by cultural heritage.

Demonstrations and observation check lists

Demonstrations of the intrapersonal standards of self-awareness, reflection, cooperation, analysis, and synthesis are more subtle than demonstrations of any of the other intelligences. It is not particularly easy to perform "reflection."

The teacher creates the list of observable behaviors by saying, "If a student were in an analytical frame of mind, what would I see and what would I hear? I would hear statements like 'Maybe that is like this' or 'I wonder what would happen if we applied this factor' or 'Could we improve the rate of speed by using larger wheels?' I would see concentration, eyes focused in thinking." In other words, verbal and visual clues help teachers know when students are involved in analyzing a situation.

These are the clues that help teachers compose the observation instruments. As they watch students working alone and in groups, they can evaluate introspective behaviors. A teacher should note how often he or she sees students engaged in the reflective activity. If the intrapersonal intelligence is a desirable intelligence to foster, teachers need to provide time for students to have silent reflective time, to engage in independent study, and to have the opportunity for self-discovery and problem solving. Observation check lists help teachers feel comfortable about giving students the time for such independent learning.

After the teacher completes this check list of observable behaviors, he or she shares it with the student. The student can use this observation of demonstrated behaviors as food for a thoughtful journal entry.

Group projects and individual projects

A project that provides for individual assessment can help students better come to know their learning styles and themselves. An excellent example of this is the "Class Reunion" activity (see page 168). This activity focuses on the student's understanding of him- or herself and calls a large group of classmates into the activity to validate each other's perceptions.

How do I align assessment with a lesson focusing on intrapersonal intelligence?

The teacher should recognize that this intelligence, just like many of the others, does not operate in isolation. Lessons can be created to help students better understand themselves and their academic goals, but the assessment can also occur using other skills from another intelligence. Consider the following lesson:

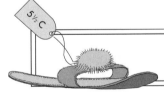

Sample Lesson: Intrapersonal

Time Capsule

TARGETED INTELLIGENCE: Intrapersonal

SUPPORTING INTELLIGENCES: Verbal/Linguistic

THINKING SKILL: Inventing, prediction

SOCIAL SKILL: Reflection as a group activity

CONTENT FOCUS: Time capsule

MATERIALS: Paper and time capsule (storage container to be designed), overhead projector or newsprint

TASK FOCUS: Making predictions

PRODUCT: Time capsule with predictions

PROBLEM: How to predict new learning

ACTIVITY:

1. Present the students with the topic of their next unit of study and have them brainstorm all they already know about the topic. List these items using an overhead projector or newsprint sheet posted at the front of the class.

2. Give pairs of students a copy of the text or other resource material they will use in the unit. Ask each pair to skim the material briefly (allowing only a few minutes) and have each student-pair predict three new ideas or facts they will learn about the topic. Make a second list of these ideas as the students announce their predictions.

3. Have students design a "time capsule," using a canister or container with a plastic resealable lid, such as a coffee can or a potato chip can. Then have the class refer to the working drafts of the two lists and design final versions for insertion in the time capsule. The capsule should then be labeled and scheduled for opening on the day before the unit test. On that day, have an "opening ceremony" and have the students go over their two lists as they review the unit.

· · · · · · · · · · · · · · · · · · · THE RUBRIC: TIME CAPSULE · · · · · · · · · · · · · · · · · · ·

Standard: Lists what will be learned in a unit and—after completing the unit—reviews predictions.

Criteria	1	2	3	4
Prior Knowledge Check	less than ten facts already learned	ten to twenty facts	twenty to thirty facts and concepts	all facts, concepts, and values already learned
Predictions of New Learnings	one fact learned	two to four facts	five to eight facts and concepts	all facts and concepts learned
Time Capsule Contents	lists explained some facts about unit	lists also decorated with key idea	personal symbols added	lists and capsule designed with overall theme

Tools: Check list; sentence stems

Comments:

_____

_____

_____

Scale
_____ = A
_____ = B
_____ = C
Below ___ = Not Yet

Final Grade: _____

How can I assess intrapersonal intelligence when it is integrated across the curriculum?

The intrapersonal intelligence is one of the easiest to assess if it is integrated across the curriculum. Teachers want to promote thoughtful, creative, critical thinkers and to do this they need to give students time to think. If the intrapersonal intelligence is made a priority in an integrated curriculum, students should have ample opportunities to reflect on what was learned from any meaningful activity in terms of both skill development and application.

Writing down a major idea or insight gained from a just-completed interaction does not take much time from the school day. But it does give a broader sense of meaning to what school is all about for students. This time for reflection crystallizes the learning experience and the insights gained. Teachers can help their students grow immeasurably by affording them the time to reflect. The few minutes spent encouraging students to "Take out your thinking logs and write down one insight you had or one question you will have or one thing you enjoyed about this activity" is well spent. What assurance students feel because they realize the activity they were involved in had merit and could be learned from and enjoyed.

Students in the primary grades who don't yet have writing skills well in hand can draw a picture about what they just experienced. When students are asked to draw at whatever age, they are being asked to use the highest-order thinking skills; they are being asked to synthesize. They are being asked to put together information so that it makes sense to them, and when the information makes sense, it is learned.

The biggest difficulty teachers have with the intrapersonal intelligence is providing time for reflection. Teachers may feel comfortable asking students to work alone. Unfortunately, all too often, when students are asked to work alone, they are being asked to fill out a work sheet of short-answer questions that do not promote any higher-level reasoning or reflection. When a teacher asks students to work alone, it should be for the purpose of independent exploration, developing problem-solving possibilities, or reflecting on what the learning process and the various activities are all about. The work that Gardner has done demonstrates that the human mind is a highly motivated learning machine that is able to understand incredibly complex concepts. The mind does this when given the opportunity to reflect, to process the connection between what is already known and that which is new information, and to internalize what it means personally. Reflection is the key to enhanced learning, and time for it needs to be built into the integrated curriculum for that curriculum to make sense.

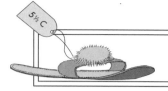

Sample Lesson: Intrapersonal

Class-Reunion Business Cards

TARGETED INTELLIGENCE: Intrapersonal

SUPPORTING INTELLIGENCES: Visual/Spatial, Verbal/Linguistic, Interpersonal

THINKING SKILL: Reviewing

SOCIAL SKILLS: Giving and getting positive feedback

CONTENT FOCUS: Self-awareness

MATERIALS: 5 × 7-inch note cards

TASK FOCUS: Designing a futuristic business card based on a lesson

PRODUCT: Business card to show during the "class reunion"

PROBLEM: How to assess one's learning of a lesson

ACTIVITY:

1. Hand out a note card to each student. On the overhead, show a model business card—one that you have already completed, showing where responses should be placed. Symbols may be used to indicate responses on the model card. Note the directions for placing the answers on the business cards are included with the questions in step 2.

2. Allow about a minute or two for each of the questions below and give students the right to pass on any of the responses. Before asking the questions, inform the students that they are making a business card that they will use to introduce themselves at a class reunion, one that is supposed to occur 10 years after this class.
   a. Center of the card: Your first name and city where you were born.
   b. Upper right corner: What is an important fact you recall from this lesson?
   c. Upper left corner: What is an important idea or concept that you recall from this lesson?
   d. Lower right corner: What did you find most interesting or boring in this lesson?
   e. Lower left corner: On a scale of 1(low) to 5 (high), rate the impact this lesson will have on events in your life after this class.

3. After the questions are answered and the business cards completed, tell the class that they are to stand up and start "mingling"—as if they were suddenly walking around at the 10-year class reunion. Each student should have his or her business card in hand. When you signal "stop," each person should introduce himself or herself to another and share the answers to questions a, b, and c. They can talk about those answers (about 20 seconds) before you ask for a remingle and then ask people to exchange responses to question d (about 60 seconds). Remingle once again to find new partners and to share responses to question e. For this last question, allow two to three minutes so that the students have time to share responses and explain why they rated the impact of the lesson as they did.

THE RUBRIC: CLASS-REUNION BUSINESS CARDS

Standard: Assesses learning through self-evaluation and dialogue.

Criteria	1	2	3	4
Completes Card According to Instructions	followed few instructions	followed some instructions	followed most instructions	followed all instructions
Reviews Key Facts	one or two facts recalled	three or four facts recalled	put multiple facts into context	related facts to several ideas
Reviews Ideas	one idea learned	one idea with several examples	more than one idea with examples	added ways to use the idea
Listens During the Reunion	interrupted with wrong questions	did not interrupt	strong eye contact	used nonverbal and verbal language to draw out others

Tools: Journals; quiz; observation check list

Comments:

_____

_____

_____

Final Grade: _____

Scale
_____ = A
_____ = B
_____ = C
Below ___ = Not Yet

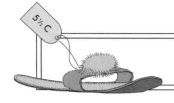

Make Your Own

TITLE: _____

TARGETED INTELLIGENCE: _Intrapersonal_ _____

SUPPORTING INTELLIGENCES: _____

THINKING SKILLS: _____

SOCIAL SKILLS: _____

CONTENT FOCUS: _____

MATERIALS: _____

TASK FOCUS: _____

PRODUCT: _____

PROBLEM: _____

ACTIVITY: _____

_____

_____

_____

_____

_____

_____

_____

_____

_____

_____

_____

_____

REFLECTIONS: _____

_____

_____

THE RUBRIC

Standard:

Criteria	1	2	3	4

Tools:

Comments:

_____

_____

_____

Final Grade: _____

Scale	
_____ = A	
_____ = B	
_____ = C	
Below ___ = Not Yet	

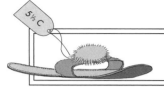

Reflection

Reflections on my assessment of intrapersonal performances:

What worked well in my classroom? _____

_____

_____

What would I like to change in my lesson and/or assessment of the lesson? _____

_____

_____

What help do I need in improving this assessment? _____

_____

_____

What are other ideas I want to try for assessing this intelligence? _____

_____

_____

Notes: _____

_____

_____

Ideas I most want to use:_____

_____

_____

_____

_____

10

Assessing Performances in Interpersonal Intelligence

What is interpersonal intelligence?

Unlike the intrapersonal intelligence, which is focused *inward*, the interpersonal intelligence focuses *outward* to other people. The most noticeable attributes of this intelligence are the abilities to understand and relate to others. Those exhibiting this intelligence notice and distinguish among others' "moods, temperaments, motivations, and intentions" (Gardner, 1983, p. 239). For example, at a very simple level, this intelligence is seen in children who notice and are sensitive to the moods of the adults around them. A more complex interpersonal skill is an adult's ablity to read the hidden intentions of others.

This intelligence includes the capacity to understand and interact with other people with a win-win result. Interpersonal intelligence involves verbal and nonverbal communication skills, collaborative skills, conflict management, consensus-building skills, and the ability to trust, respect, lead, and motivate others to the achievement of a *mutually* beneficial goal. Empathy for feelings, fears, anticipations, and beliefs of others; the willingness to listen without judgment; and the desire to help others raise their level of performance to its highest are all critical traits of those with a strong interpersonal intelligence.

Why is interpersonal intelligence important in the curriculum?

As we move from the factory model of education where students learn discrete facts by rote memory toward a classroom of socially shared learning, this intelligence becomes critical. Ever-increasing numbers of the world's businesses and industries encourage whole-team participation in product design, development, and production. As the globe shrinks and more and more cultures come into daily contact through electronic communication, this intelligence helps individuals interact across cultural and language barriers. To prepare students to successfully move into these interactive business environments, curriculum models need to provide a variety of collaborative, interactive learning activities that develop interpersonal skills.

What classroom practices develop interpersonal intelligence?

In a fifth grade classroom outside of Boston, students work in groups to create a spaceship that will take them to an undiscovered planet in the galaxy. As part of their small-group assignment, students decide which group members will assume the following roles: captain, navigator, nutritionist, and technical engineer. Three groups out of eight select educationally challenged students to assume the role of "captain." The group members recognize certain traits in these infused learning-disabled (LD) students that transcend their label. These students are learning how to build on the strengths that all members bring to the cooperative group. They are learning to come to consensus about what characteristics best define a captain, an engineer, a navigator, or a nutritionist, and they are learning how to build the collaborative skills that will aid them in creating a successful product to take them on their journey into space.

In a high school tech-prep class in Michigan, students divide themselves into groups to design low-income housing for the homeless. The division of responsibility is made recognizing the desired skills for each job. The groups of four include an artistic draftsperson, an engineering whiz, a practical mathematician, and a materials organizer. In this context, these students are learning the value of divergent skills working together to produce a better product. Like workers in the innovative Saturn plants, these students experience many hands becoming one.

What standards could a teacher use to develop a rubric for interpersonal intelligence?

Teamwork

This standard best represents the essence of the interpersonal intelligence. The team that works together recognizes that the sum of their combined efforts is greater than what any one individual could accomplish alone. As the team encourages development of the individual talents of each member, it recognizes its strengths and celebrates its accomplishments. True teamwork is demonstrated in the attitude that "we are all in this together" and with our united efforts, we can accomplish the assigned task. There are no loafers or directors on a team; there is cooperation and respect for the individual talents that compose the team. The ultimate goal is an outstanding product, performance, or demonstration that represents the quality of team interdependence.

Cooperative problem solving

The interpersonal intelligence manifests itself in cooperative problem solving. When a group of students functions well together, they share ideas about ways to approach a problem. As they create their list of strategies, the atmosphere is one of support for the variety of ideas. Encouragement is given in statements such as, "Is there anything else we need to consider?" or "What is another possibility?" or "What else could we do here?" Students demonstrate cooperative problem solving when they create a low-risk environment where they comfortably share as many options as possible and then judiciously prioritize the options proposed as they search for the best solutions.

Encouragement

A strong aspect of the interpersonal intelligence is the ability to encourage others. This is done through encouraging peers to take the risk of explaining a personal point of view, to think more deeply about a situation, to stretch in making connections, or to stay on task until the job is finished. The encourager demonstrates respect for others' opinions by giving verbal and nonverbal support to others to accept difficult challenges and overcome obstinate barriers.

Consensus seeking

Students with this intelligence prefer to collaborate on tasks because they dislike working alone. They recognize that to accomplish the group's assignment, an understanding needs to be reached about how to achieve the final goal. Students who demonstrate this standard achieve consensus by having the group talk things over, lay out the options, and establish how the group product or performance will be presented. This demonstrable standard is different from cooperative problem solving, because it requires a great deal more facilitation. The group consensus seeker artfully moves the group members through an understanding of the different options presented and helps everyone decide which strategies best fit the group's common goal.

What is a sample rubric for interpersonal intelligence?

In the primary grades, the put-down sometimes becomes an art form. Unsure of their own strengths and often overwhelmed by competitive pressures, young students try to outdo each other using negative remarks that insult their peers. To counter this, an essential performance standard is the use of praise or recognition of others' accomplishments.

THE RUBRIC

The Standard: Giving recognition to others

THE CRITERIA

High Performance: Student always uses affirming words about the quality of the group's work and the ability of each member to stay on task.

Sound Performance: Student frequently gives verbal support as the group works to complete an assignment.

Adequate Performance: Student sometimes gives verbal or nonverbal support for contributions to the group.

Not Yet: Student does not share any positive comments when working with a partner or in a group. Is argumentative and often demeans work of others in a group.

To help reinforce this standard, the posted rubric may contain a list of positive ways to praise group members that does not sound artificial. These indicators should come from the students after they brainstorm a list of acceptable ways to praise one another. By creating this list, students better understand how positive recognition creates a safe environment for collaboration. At the various grade levels, the indicator lists may vary.

Primary indicators might include the following:

HAPPY TALK

Looks Like	Sounds Like
Smile	Good job
Head nod	Way to go
Thumbs up	Yes!!!!
Pat on the back	I like your answer.

In the upper grades, the cooperative social skill of consensus seeking is a challenge. As students work on group tasks, the posted rubric in standard format can remind them of ways to develop this skill, which will play such an important role in their work lives.

THE RUBRIC

The Standard: Seeking Consensus

THE CRITERIA

High Performance: Student helps group recognize the different ideas presented and encourages group acceptance of one.
    Indicators: "I'm not clear yet on what you mean."
        "I think what you are saying is. . . . Am I right?"
        "We have two different ideas on the table. Let's see what they have in common."
        "We have to come up with one best answer. How can we do that?"
        "Let's remember our common goal. What ideas will get us there?"

Sound Performance: Student can explain the different ideas and with group tries to figure out how to proceed.
    Indicators: "Let me summarize."
        "Let's make connections."
        "Let's plan our next steps."

Adequate Performance: Student encourages re-explanation of ideas shared.
    Indicators: "Could you run that by us one more time?"
        "What other ways can we say that?"

Not Yet: Insists his or her idea is best and refuses to compromise.
    Indicators: "That's stupid."
        "Oh, come on."
        "No way, man."

To advance their development, reformat the rubric into the more practical matrix style, as follows:

THE RUBRIC: GIVING RECOGNITION

Standard: Recognizes by positive comments the achievements of others.

Criteria	1	2	3	4
Affirming Words	seldom praises	praises aren't specific	uses "I" message with specifics	uses "I" message with specifics and personal acclaim
Encouragement	shakes head up and down	makes one encouraging statement	makes two encouraging statements	makes three or more encouraging statements
Body Language	smiles	nods head and smiles	uses smiles and other behaviors	uses smiles, pats on back appropriately

Tools: Observation check list

Comments:

_____

_____

_____

Final Grade: _____

Scale

_____ = A

_____ = B

_____ = C

Below ___ = Not Yet

Posted rubrics are especially effective for encouraging practice of the interpersonal skills. As students work in the groups, individuals can do a quick check to see what words or actions will move the group task forward. As the students experience the right and wrong uses of the social skills involved in interaction, they gain confidence in using the appropriate actions and words for different collaborative situations.

What assessment tools are most useful for interpersonal intelligence?

The student with this intelligence responds to a "we" atmosphere in the classroom. A great way to get this student's attention is to start a lesson with the think-pair-share strategy such as: "Think what we know about. . . . Now, turn to your partner and share what you already know." The interpersonal student also enjoys instruction organized through cooperative study groups, base groups, group investigations, group games and activities, informal pair-sharing, team projects, and pair tutors.

To construct an interactive classroom where development of the interpersonal intelligence is purposeful, teachers need to see themselves as facilitators of interactive learning. They will have to teach the cooperative social skills, model their use, and set up learning tasks that require the students to practice and to assess use of the targeted social skills. As students work in groups, teachers monitor how well students perform their assigned roles, cooperate with others, and complete the group task. The assessment tool that can be most helpful in this group learning environment is the observation check list.

Observation check lists

During the first weeks of school, the teacher uses informal group sharing to introduce cooperative skills, such as attentive listening and looking at the speaker. As the teacher works with students to understand the guidelines for cooperative group behavior, he or she is assessing the level of their interpersonal skills. Students need these skills for cooperative learning to occur: attentive listening, teamwork, giving encouragement, and celebrating accomplishments. More advanced cooperative social skills include clarifying, solving conflicts, and creating consensus.

When the teacher has determined which social skills the students need to work on, he or she will create observation check lists to help validate student growth in the use of skills. Check lists could include:

PRIMARY EXAMPLES

- Uses six-inch voice
- Listens to partner
- Stays with the group
- Looks at the speaker
- Is sensitive to others' feelings

MIDDLE GRADE EXAMPLES

- Uses quiet voice
- Does not interrupt others
- Helps others
- Performs the role assigned
- Listens to all ideas
- Looks for more than one answer
- Encourages others

SECONDARY EXAMPLES

- Controls voice level
- Thinks for him- or herself
- Respects others' opinions/ideas
- Helps the group stay on task
- Is a responsible group member
- Helps explore different points of view
- Includes all group members

OBSERVER'S CHECKLIST				
Desired Social Skill	Group A	Group B	Group C	Group D
1				
2				
3				
4				

Bellanca & Fogarty (1991, p. 295)

Demonstrations

Demonstrations can be a powerful way for students to show the positive results of cooperative interaction. They also validate the learning and sharing that occurred in the group's activities. The criteria for the demonstration are set before the group begins to work together. To ensure success, students need to understand what is expected for high performance. The teacher and students agree on the length of the demonstration, appropriate visuals, costumes, what the dialogue should include, and what props will be needed. Class time is provided for students to create and practice their demonstrations. As the students are involved in their preparations, the teacher monitors to be certain that students are clear on their roles and everyone is sharing in the task. When the demonstration moment arrives, the students could be videotaped and copies put in their portfolios.

In the interpersonal arena, both direct and indirect demonstrations of social skills are valuable. Using the direct approach, the teacher asks the students to demonstrate a real-life work situation where they must use the targeted social skill. For instance, primary students may set up role plays showing how encouragement might look and sound among employees in a toy store or for the seven dwarfs at work in the mine. Middle grade students might role-play or make a video showing how to resolve a disagreement with a dissatisfied customer in a department store.

Using the indirect approach, the teacher would structure his or her assessment of a content demonstration so that students know he or she is assessing both their knowledge of the content and their ability to use the targeted social skill. For instance, a P.E. teacher might ask student pairs to demonstrate how to teach a third child to shoot a free throw. The teacher would note what the children know about the technique and how they go about giving encouragement.

Teacher-made tests

One way for teachers to monitor the learning that occurs in cooperative groups is to create brief test items that check for understanding and transfer. After doing a demonstration, for example, a teacher could ask the students to explain what they had learned and where this learning could be useful. In the interpersonal learning environment, teacher-made tests help to focus on the issues of group dynamics and problem-solving skills. Standard tests that test for content can certainly be used in this learning environment. The content has not changed; what has changed is how the students are being taught the content.

Here is a sample test on cooperative social skills.

1. What adjectives best describe a person who is cooperative?

2. What are some words a person might use to encourage you?

3. Why is it important to encourage each other at work?

Logs and journals

In the interpersonal learning environment, logs and journals are probably more effective as processing tools than as assessment tools. At the end of a cooperative activity, for example, a teacher may ask students to take out their reflective journals and consider how their teamwork went and what teamwork skills they think they are developing. Or he or she may ask students to record two new insights they made and one question they still have. If these thinking logs are maintained on a daily basis, students can go back and review their insights and questions before being tested on the content. When some of their questions are still unanswered, they can review, first with a learning buddy and then with the entire class.

Group projects

Projects completed in cooperative groups provide several elements for assessment. In Madison, Wisconsin, middle grade students elected to find out what Madison might look like in the year 2020. The ultimate goal was to create a diorama done to scale of the city in the year 2020. Students surveyed all the middle grade students and their parents in the Madison area. The goal of the survey was demographic. Where were people expecting to live in the year 2020?

To help the students successfully accomplish their tasks, the project was *chunked*. Each chunk represented a percentage of the total grade and provided opportunity for individual assessment as well. For example, the first chunk was the creation of the survey instruments for the two different populations. Students and teachers created standards for clear, concise questions with answers that could be keyed into a data base. Each group of students developed four questions with written explanations about their choices. Based on the criteria set for the questions, they were evaluated on a percentage basis. The students also received individual grades for their written defense of the questions they wrote for the surveys.

Students then prioritized the questions and came to consensus about which ones to use. When the surveys came back, students keyed in the data and ran a statistical analysis. Groups decided what the data meant for the future demographics of Madison and individually defended their decisions. The project moved forward through the series of stages outlined by the students and teachers until the actual diorama was completed. Benchmarks and time lines were established across the project. Everyone was clear on the project's scope, steps, and outcomes. Individual assessments were built into each step and provided teachers with definable, defensible assessments. Needless to say, all the students demonstrated high levels of understanding and success.

Interviews

Interviews are a useful assessment tool in an interpersonal learning environment. In fact, informal interviews occur daily. When students finish their cooperative task, most often they are asked: What did you do to work as a team? Where else can you use these team-building skills? Other informal questions include: What was your job? How well did you do your job? What might your group need to work on? What did you do well? What might you do differently the next time?

The more formal interview most often occurs when a teacher wants to find out more about how an individual student views the cooperative interaction. Such questions might include: Can you tell me how your group work is going? Is there something you particularly like? Is there some difficulty you are having? What are you learning from the conversations in your group? The teacher is listening for an understanding of the cooperative environment and the comfort level the student has with it.

How do I align assessment with a lesson focusing on interpersonal intelligence?

Embedding interpersonal skills in every learning task is a beneficial goal for several reasons. First, when students practice cooperative social skills in their daily interaction, the teacher has fewer management and discipline issues to worry about. Most discipline problems arise from students who cannot interact in positive ways with the teacher or their peers. The teacher has the option of constantly putting out these fires or of encouraging students to take responsibility for communicating in positive ways. By teaching and assessing cooperative social skills, the teacher can diminish his or her involvement in discipline and increase all the students' involvement in positive interactions.

Lessons that teach the desired social skills are the start. Direct instruction introduces the standard, explains the importance of the interpersonal intelligence in a here-and-now context, the classroom, and models the best use of the skill. After this first lesson, the teacher integrates the social skill into all content lessons and conducts regular assessments on the students' increasing proficiency. His or her high expectations, based on the understanding that he or she will reteach and give regular feedback, is that all the students will seek to meet the high performance standard.

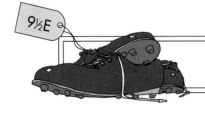

Sample Lesson: Interpersonal

Dialogue

TARGETED INTELLIGENCE: Interpersonal

SUPPORTING INTELLIGENCES: Visual/Spatial, Intrapersonal

THINKING SKILLS: Generating ideas, selecting from alternatives

SOCIAL SKILLS: Teamwork, cooperative problem solving

CONTENT FOCUS: Teamwork based on mutual agreements

MATERIALS: Posterboard, markers

TASK FOCUS: Use guidelines to ensure all parties agree on behaviors appropriate to a safe discussion.

PRODUCT: None

PROBLEM: How to develop group agreements

ACTIVITY:

1. On newsprint, a bulletin board, or duplicated handout, provide the acronym: DIALOGUE.

Guidelines for Dialogue

Defer judgment.
Inquire about ideas; don't interrogate individuals.
Ask open-ended questions about your concerns.
Look for areas of agreement.
Offer a different perspective.
Grab the focus issue.
Use your strengths.
Express your appreciation.

---

2. Read the meaning of each letter and ask students "why" they think each is important for a "safe" classroom discussion. Seek at least two ideas for each letter—phrase by asking for different interpretations or for others to add to the first answer. After discussion of the "E," ask for two or three summaries of the entire word. Close with a discussion of how DIALOGUE guidelines would benefit class discussions.
3. Post the DIALOGUE guidelines. Ask each group to select 4 items from the content of a group rubric. After a group task, instruct the groups to self-assess via the group rubric.

THE RUBRIC: DIALOGUE

Standard: Uses selected guidelines during group discussion.

Criteria	1	2	3	4
Defers Judgment	negative comments	silent	comments positively but interrupts	comments positively and appropriately
Open-Ended Questions	asks for facts	paraphrases questions	clarifies questions if asked	asks "what if" questions
Different Perspectives	self-centered	one point of view	explores at least two views	seeks multiple views
Appreciation	negative	praises in general	praises specifics	praises and encourages

Tools: Observation check list

Comments:

_____

_____

_____

Final Grade: _____

Scale

_____ = A

_____ = B

_____ = C

Below ___ = Not Yet

FURTHER INSTRUCTIONS:

1. The direct lesson is the start. As students proceed into the curriculum, the teacher will expect that they practice and refine the target skill whenever he or she structures a collaborative lesson. For instance, in a middle grade science lesson on buoyancy, the team may have the tasks of reading the explanation of buoyancy and then placing a pumpkin, a rock, and a paper cup in a tub of water. After the students complete the experiment, they

are to agree on conclusions so that each student can write a paper about what they learned about buoyancy. In addition, the group is asked to assess how it worked as a team. Finally, each student is asked to assess his or her own teamwork and attach a written summary to the buoyancy paper. For the team assessment, the teacher reviews the teamwork rubric.

2. With older students, the teacher may want to put a greater emphasis on the interpersonal skills. For instance, in a ninth grade English task, a Colorado teacher uses the writing curriculum as an opportunity to integrate the social skills within her writing assignments. Because she uses cooperative base groups each week for peer editing, she insists that they develop goals for improving how they work together. Midway through the writing curriculum, one of her assignments is an essay that focuses on the student teams' goal setting. The rubric for team goal setting may look like this:

THE RUBRIC: TEAMWORK

Standard: Demonstrates use of teamwork skills in a team-based lesson.

Criteria	1	2	3	4
Responsibility for Job	sporadic	does at minimum	does with consistency	does and assesses plus/minus
Active Listening	quiet	focuses eyes on speaker	asks appropriate questions	checks out statements with paraphrase
Contributor of Content	answers questions	identifies and summarizes	explains key points	guides inquiry at the right time
Encouragement	praises	encourages one person	encourages all	creates encouraging atmosphere

Tools: Plus/Minus chart; sentence stems; group observation chart

Comments:

_____

_____

Final Grade: _____

Scale	
_____	= A
_____	= B
_____	= C
Below ___	= Not Yet

How can I assess interpersonal intelligence when it is integrated across the curriculum?

Of all the intelligences, the interpersonal is the easiest to assess if it is integrated across the curriculum. Integrating interpersonal intelligence requires the teacher to move away from total direct instruction, often described as the "sage on the stage," to a wide range of student-centered, interactive groupings. The room should be set up to encourage the interpersonal intelligence. When the classroom desks are organized into small, clustered work stations and cooperative guidelines are prominently posted, interactive thinking is encouraged on a daily basis.

If this intelligence is integrated across the curriculum, it will be demonstrated in so many positive ways. Students will be involved in group activities ranging from peer editing to group investigation. Students will talk, some excitedly, some more controlled, and the teacher will be difficult to spot because he or she will be involved in one of the group discussions. The atmosphere will exude warmth and encourage the free flow of ideas. Students and teachers will react in respectful ways. Students will reinforce and support one another. Attendance will improve and discipline problems will diminish. The faculty will experience collegiality.

If a school's goal is to integrate the curriculum through the multiple intelligences, one of the easiest ways to begin is to honor and employ the interpersonal intelligence throughout the learning environment.

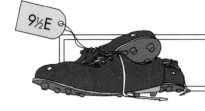

Sample Lesson: Interpersonal

Generational Interviews

TARGETED INTELLIGENCE: Interpersonal

SUPPORTING INTELLIGENCES: Verbal/Linguistic, Visual/Spatial

THINKING SKILLS: Inquiry, analysis

SOCIAL SKILLS: Respect for elders, active listening

CONTENT FOCUS: Respect for elders

MATERIALS: Notepads, newsprint, markers

TASK FOCUS: To interview an adult at least one generation removed

PRODUCT: Class Venn diagram comparing intergenerational views

PROBLEM: How to understand and to respect elder's views

ACTIVITY:

1. Use a KWL chart (What we think we *know*, what we *want* to know, what we *learned*) with the whole class to identify what they think they know about their grandparents' or great grandparents' lives and what they want to learn.

2. Let the class know that they are going to be team reporters interviewing senior citizens about their generation's growing-up experiences.

3. Using the want to know list, make a questionnaire and distribute it to teams of two.

4. Practice with the teams *how* to ask the questions with respect and caring.

5. Arrange for the class to go on a field trip to a senior home. Let the seniors know what will be happening.

6. If you have a video camera, videotape some of the interviews. Be sure the students use their interview notebooks to record their answers.

7. When the students return to the classroom, use the L on the KWL chart to guide the discussion: "What did you learn through the interviews?"

8. Make an all-class Venn on the blackboard to compare and contrast the generational views.

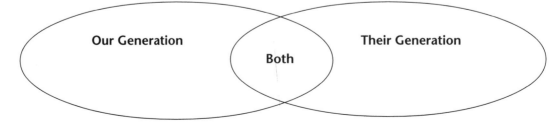

REFLECTIONS: Use student journals. Here are possible lead-ins:
- What surprised me about the ideas shared?
- What did I learn about respecting elders' views?
- How will I be a better person for what I learned?

THE RUBRIC: GENERATIONAL INTERVIEW

Standard: Shows respect for elders during an interview.

Criteria	1	2	3	4
Rationale for Behavior	weak explanation	one to two valid reasons	three to four valid reasons	three to four valid reasons with examples
Active Listening	eye contact	eye contact, head nods	eye contact, head nods, smiles	eye contact, head nods, smiles, appropriate questions
Patience	seems not to listen to elders	listens but does not respond	listens and responds	listens and encourages
Feeling Tone	acceptance of situation	acceptance of person	some caring shown	genuine warmth expressed

Tools: Observation check list; video camera

Comments:

_____

_____

_____

Scale
_____ = A
_____ = B
_____ = C
Below ___ = Not Yet

Final Grade: _____

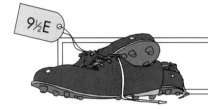

Make Your Own

TITLE: _____

TARGETED INTELLIGENCE: _Interpersonal_ _____

SUPPORTING INTELLIGENCES: _____

THINKING SKILLS: _____

SOCIAL SKILLS: _____

CONTENT FOCUS: _____

MATERIALS: _____

TASK FOCUS: _____

PRODUCT: _____

PROBLEM: _____

ACTIVITY: _____

_____

_____

_____

_____

_____

_____

_____

_____

_____

_____

_____

REFLECTIONS: _____

_____

_____

············· THE RUBRIC ·············

Standard:

Criteria	1	2	3	4

Tools:

Comments:

_____

_____

_____

Final Grade: _____

Scale
_____ = A
_____ = B
_____ = C
Below ___ = Not Yet

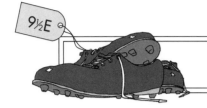

Reflection

Reflection on my assessment of interpersonal performances:

What worked well in my classroom? _____

_____

_____

What would I like to change in my lesson and/or assessment of the lesson? _____

_____

_____

Where do I need help in improving the assessment? _____

_____

_____

What are other ideas I want to try for assessing this intelligence? _____

_____

_____

Notes: _____

_____

_____

Ideas I most want to use:_____

_____

_____

_____

_____

_____

11

Assessing Performances in Naturalist Intelligence

What is naturalist intelligence?

This intelligence, which Howard Gardner added to his original seven in 1995, springs from an individual's ability to recognize species of plants or animals in his or her environment and to create taxonomies that classify the many different subspecies. Individuals such as Charles Darwin, John Audubon, Louis Agassiz, and E. O. Wilson are well-known naturalists. Young children who can pick out different types of flowers, name different types of animals, or arrange such common items as shoes, cars, or designer clothes into common categories are budding naturalists.

The connection to naturalistic knowing is obvious in botany and zoology, but individuals who work with organic chemistry, entomology, medicine, photography, civil engineering, and a host of other fields must also develop their naturalist skills.

Why is the naturalist intelligence important in the curriculum?

This intelligence is essential to high performance in the study of science. Starting in the early grades with the study of patterns, the examination of the characteristics of a community, and the introduction to hands-on science activities, the science curriculum proceeds to in-depth studies of biology, earth science, and chemistry with regular and advanced placement courses. Success in these courses is often a gate to careers in engineering, science, and medicine.

What classroom practices develop naturalist intelligence?

Hands-on science experiments

The literature on science performances spotlights the importance of hands-on, active experiences in the study of science. In the early grades, this may mean that science study starts with gathering leaves in the fall. The students then group their findings according to the common characteristics they see. In the middle grades, it can mean that students gather water samples, use microscopes to find similar algae, and then label their findings. In biology, it can mean examining and classifying cells from many sources. Reading about a science topic and then watching a movie to learn about a species are not included in this approach.

Logs and journals with thought-producing questions

Two basic tools for a scientist are the log and the journal. The log is used for recording observations and making on-the-spot notes. The journal is a tool for recording day-to-day reflections, making sketches, and dreaming of new ideas. (Older students can study the journals of Charles Darwin and Leonardo da Vinci.) A teacher developing the habits of mind that are part of the naturalist intelligence will use logs and journals on a regular basis. Each time students are involved in observing a phenomenon, the teacher will ask them to jot their observations in the log. Several times a week she may ask them to reflect on what they have been learning about the natural world in the journal, sketch new ideas, or use graphic organizers to display their thinking about the natural world.

Graphic organizers

Graphic organizers that lend themselves to naturalist thinking and acting are the web, the Venn diagram, and the matrix. The web helps students identify the attributes or characteristics of an individual or species. The Venn diagram enables students to make visually organized comparisons of individuals, species, or families with specific clarification of similarities and differences. The matrix allows students to classify and categorize by attribute. All three organizers encourage the naturalist ways of thinking, specifically classifying and categorizing in many different disciplines. For instance, language arts students studying characters in a novel can use the organizers to identify common attributes and make a detailed comparison with the help of the Venn diagram.

Projects

Projects are a "natural" way to develop the naturalist intelligence, especially if the project follows scientific methods for gathering information, making sense of the information, and assessing the results. They also allow for the integration of such strategies as hands-on experiments and graphic organizers. Projects are more complex than experiments and often cover several weeks. Projects that fail to ask students to reflect on what they are doing and understand how they obtained the project's results are little more than activities. When students must use logs, journals, and other reflective tools in order to think about what they are learning, the projects become a valuable tool for promoting naturalists' learning. When projects take advantage of the naturalist way of knowing across the intelligences (e.g., an art project that shows pencil shading of three to five coniferous forms), other intelligences are enriched.

Problems

Gardner's explanation of an intelligence as a problem-solving process is easily accomplished in the naturalist way of knowing through problem-based learning. In this method, the teacher presents a problem for the students to solve. The problem may involve the amount of pollution in a stream or the accumulation of hazardous waste materials in a community. The more connected the problem is to the everyday experiences of the students the better. Using their basic skills—reading, mathematics, thinking, etc.— students must call on their knowledge or find new information to help them solve the problem. As they progress through the inquiry process, the teacher will ask the types of questions that mediate the development of the students' naturalist intelligence.

What standards could a teacher use to develop a rubric for naturalist intelligence?

Accuracy

Effective scientific thought relies on accurate observation of detail. This accuracy comes from intense concentration of the senses in noting all that is seen and heard.

Precision

Taxonomies are derived from clear, exact distinctions that separate one object from another. Unless there is great care in making these very fine distinctions, the conclusions made will be faulty.

Logic

The naturalist intelligence thrives on the development of convergent, logical thinking through the identification and classification of common attributes, the categorization of species, and deductive reasoning.

Persistence

A characteristic often assigned to the most successful scientists is their ability to try over and over again to find the answer to a question by the slight alteration of a single element in an experiment. Some scientists, like Jonas Salk, work for years to find the verification of their hypotheses. The true naturalist learns never to give up.

What is a sample rubric for naturalist intelligence?

THE RUBRIC: NATURALIST INTELLIGENCE

Standard: Shows ability to make a precise classification of attributes of a given phenomenon.

Criteria	1	2	3	4
Labels	85–89% correct	90–94% correct	95–99% correct	100% correct
Multiple Attributes	one attribute	two attributes	three attributes	four attributes
Precise Examples	two or three examples	four to five examples	six to seven examples	eight examples
Differentiation	70–79% correct	80–89% correct	90–99% correct	100% correct

Tools: Teacher-made test

Comments:

_____

_____

_____

Final Grade: _____

Scale

_____ = A

_____ = B

_____ = C

Below ___ = Not Yet

What assessment tools are most useful for naturalist intelligence?

Observation check lists

The naturalist thinker begins with a hypothesis. Next, she builds a check list for the observable data she believes will present itself. As she observes, she marks off each piece of data in the appropriate column. The classroom teacher who wants to model the naturalist's way of thinking will use check lists to help students track what they are doing in the classroom.

Logs

For the naturalist, the log is an open-ended tool for observing and recording data. Once she has amassed enough data, she begins to make judgments that will verify or deny her hypothesis. Students can use logs to track their own progress in a naturalist fashion.

How do I align assessment with a lesson focusing on naturalist intelligence?

As demonstrated in the other intelligences, a useful assessment begins with a lesson, unit, or project that requires students to perform the skills involved in this way of thinking.

Sample Lesson: Naturalist

Cellular Debate

TARGETED INTELLIGENCE: Naturalist

SUPPORTING INTELLIGENCES: Interpersonal, Visual/Spatial, Verbal/Linguistic

THINKING SKILL: Classifying

SOCIAL SKILL: Listening to other points of view

CONTENT FOCUS: Science; biology (cells)

MATERIALS: Newsprint, markers

TASK FOCUS: After studying the parts of the cell, mixed-ability student groups will prepare a defense of their part of the cell as being the most important. Each student in the group must take part in the presentation of the initial argument and in the rebuttals.

PRODUCT: Picture of a cell with its parts labeled and the group's position recorded

PROBLEM: How to determine the most important part of the cell

ACTIVITY:
1. After completing the study of the cell, assign students into mixed-ability groups. For each group, assign one part (e.g., cell wall, nucleus, etc.) to defend as the most important part of the cell.
2. Allow groups twenty minutes to prepare arguments. Set ground rules and criteria for debate first.
3. Allow ten minutes for initial presentations by each group. Do a round-robin rebuttal. If possible, use outside observers such as parents or other teachers to judge the debate and select the winning group.

REFLECTIONS:
1. What did you learn about the cell from this debate?
2. What did you contribute to your group's assignment as far as using logic and precise thought were concerned?

THE RUBRIC: CELLULAR DEBATE

Standard: Shows understanding of the parts of a cell.

Criteria	1	2	3	4
Examples Labeled	70–79% correct	80–89% correct	90–99% correct	100% correct
Process	knows cell functions	explains value of each part	relates cell function to life functions	defends importance of each element
Knowledge of Cell	knows 80–89% of parts	knows 90–99% of parts	explains all parts (100%)	knows relationships among parts
Logical Argument	correct answer; wrong logic	conclusion follows logical rules	universal statement and examples align	follows all criteria for debate

Tools: Lab test; test; check list

Comments:

_____

_____

_____

Final Grade: _____

Scale	
_____	= A
_____	= B
_____	= C
Below ___	= Not Yet

How can I assess naturalist intelligence when it is integrated across the curriculum?

Studies in the naturalist mode may provide the best opportunity for integrated study. If the teacher sets up a problem-based performance in science, such as an investigation of a local wildlife problem, the student will call upon a variety of intelligences to get the solution.

For instance, consider the problem of expanding deer populations in suburban forest preserves. The teacher can design a multidisciplinary unit that requires the students to (1) read about the problem and write a summary of what has been done in other cities; (2) interview rangers from the local preserve and citizens who live adjacent to the preserve; (3) stake out and photograph the deer; (4) gather samples of damaged flora and fauna and classify each species on a chart; (5) conduct a debate or make a visual presentation on the findings.

To assess this unit, the teacher has many options: (1) grade, according to a rubric, the written summary, the interview questions, the photographs, the classification chart, and the debate or chart; (2) assign a value to each grade that is added into a final grade; (3) use an observation chart to record each student's contributions to group tasks; (4) require a self-assessment essay and grade it according to a rubric.

Sample Lesson: Naturalist

Classifying Local Flowers

TARGETED INTELLIGENCE: Naturalist

SUPPORTING INTELLIGENCES: Visual/Spatial, Verbal/Linguistic

THINKING SKILL: Classifying

SOCIAL SKILL: Sharing

CONTENT FOCUS: Science; botany (flowers)

MATERIALS: Glue, pencil, construction paper

TASK FOCUS: Pairs of students collect sample flowers and arrange them in a 3 × 3 matrix

PRODUCT: Matrix with classified flower samples

PROBLEM: How to distinguish different flowers

ACTIVITY:
1. Match students in pairs and give each pair a set of materials.
2. Instruct each student to gather nine flowers in sets of three.
3. Invite the students to make a 3 × 3 inch matrix on the construction paper and glue the flowers in three vertical columns and three horizontal columns. After the students glue the flowers, instruct them to label the horizontal and vertical columns with a common attribute.
4. Sign and post the completed works.

REFLECTIONS:
Ask each group to explain its labels and explain what was difficult about the task. Mediate responses so that all labels are correct. Use the following rubric for assessment.

THE RUBRIC: CLASSIFYING LOCAL FLOWERS

Standard: Students collect and categorize using a 3 × 3 matrix.

Criteria	1	2	3	4
Labels Align	less than 70% align	80% align	90% align	all labels align
Examples Align	less than 70% align	80% align	90% align	all examples align
Reasons Provided for Placements	reasons provided not valid	valid reasons provided for 80–89%	valid reasons provided for 90–99%	two valid reasons provided for all placements (100%)

Tools:

Comments:

_____

_____

_____

Final Grade: _____

Scale

_____ = A

_____ = B

_____ = C

Below ___ = Not Yet

Make Your Own

TITLE : _____

TARGETED INTELLIGENCE: _Naturalist_____

SUPPORTING INTELLIGENCES: _____

THINKING SKILLS: _____

SOCIAL SKILLS: _____

CONTENT FOCUS: _____

MATERIALS: _____

TASK FOCUS: _____

PRODUCT: _____

PROBLEM: _____

ACTIVITY _____

_____

_____

_____

_____

_____

_____

_____

_____

_____

_____

_____

_____

REFLECTIONS: _____

_____

_____

- THE RUBRIC -

Standard:

Criteria	1	2	3	4

Tools:

Comments:

_____

_____

_____

Final Grade: _____

Scale

_____ = A

_____ = B

_____ = C

Below ___ = Not Yet

Reflection

Reflections on my assessment of naturalist performances:

What worked well in my classroom? _____

_____

_____

What would I like to change in my lesson and/or assessment of the lesson? _____

_____

_____

What help do I need in improving this assessment? _____

_____

_____

What are other ideas I want to try for assessing this intelligence? _____

_____

_____

Notes: _____

_____

_____

Ideas I most want to use: _____

_____

_____

_____

_____

_____

12

Creating a Multiple Intelligences Portfolio

What is a portfolio?

A portfolio is a collection of exemplary work. Architects, painters and sculptors, and art students have long used the portfolio for transporting samples of their best work. Today, computer graphic designers, filmmakers, actors, scientists, and stockbrokers use the portfolio to organize the artifacts of their daily work. Whether seeking a patron, applying for a job, preparing for a show, or organizing tax returns, the portfolio is a convenient tool for collecting and carrying samples of what one can do.

The portfolio is first and foremost a collection bin for organizing the artifacts of an individual's work or school life. As an assessment tool, portfolios predate the current grading system. Before letter grades became popular at the turn of the century, the portfolio was the tool that told students and parents how well a student was performing in class. In the one-room schoolhouses of pre-factory school days, children used crates and boxes for storing their slates and samples of the work they did in learning the basic skills or in making a project for social studies or art. During conferences, the teacher or the child would share the child's portfolio of work with the parents.

In the business world, the portfolio is often the tool used in performance reviews. When it is time for the annual performance review, the manager invites the employee to prepare a self-assessment for the year. The well-organized employee keeps samples of important work done. A novice lawyer may select documents from the two cases he or she won in court. A civil engineer might include photos of the diagrams and blueprints of a construction project he or she supervised. A stockbroker may include charts of his or her clients' stock performance. A graphic artist could include sample video renderings of his or her multimedia ad work. With the best examples as a guide, these employees prepare a written self-evaluation describing what they have accomplished during the year. Before the performance review, the manager considers the portfolio with the employee's self-evaluation as a guide.

If applicants for a job need a way to grab the attention of the personnel director, they might include a miniportfolio with their resumes. When they return for the second interview, they get the upper hand by bringing along a portfolio of their best work. This separates them from the many others seeking the same job.

As teachers elect to teach using the framework of the multiple intelligences, they quickly see how to expand the possible ways they can assess student learning. Instead of relying solely on standardized and teacher-made tests, they see the many uses of observation check lists, essays, journals, logs, exhibits of art work, short stories, demonstrations, model building, interviews, and performances. In order to keep the best of each student's work well organized in classrooms with 20 to 36 primary students or 125 to 150 high schoolers, these teachers use the multiple intelligences portfolio.

A well-constructed portfolio is an excellent, easy-to-use tool for students in the multiple intelligences classroom. To be useful to the teacher, students, and parents who are concerned about performing with quality, the well-constructed portfolio should meet certain standards. What are those standards?

A well-made classroom portfolio, whether in primary, middle, or secondary school, is organized, selective, representative, and promotes insight.

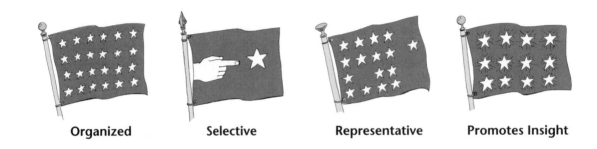

Organized   **Selective**   **Representative**   **Promotes Insight**

Organized

A quality portfolio is *organized* for easy access. Like a safety deposit box in a bank vault, it comprises the student's most valuable work for the year, indexed and labeled for prompt review. Like a museum, it presents each artist's work so that the viewer focuses on the quality of the artist's achievement.

Paris' Picasso Museum exemplifies the museum as portfolio. When visitors enter the vestibule of the reconstructed mansion, they first see a giant floor plan of the museum. Donated to the French government in lieu of the large estate taxes owed by the Picasso family, the museum is organized according to decades—including the artist's life, times, and artistic periods. Selected pieces of Picasso's pottery, diary, sketches, sculptures, and paintings are arranged chronologically from room to room. In each room, visitors are greeted with a photo display of the major historic events of the decade, photos of Picasso and his family and friends, and a brief essay in English and French that links the artist's life and works of the ten-year period with the social and artistic influences he experienced. A second essay focuses on the major works in the room. This essay describes Picasso's dominant styles of the decade and highlights the best works in the room that represent those styles.

As visitors follow the guided path from room to room and decade to decade, the photo and essay displays reveal the essential themes of Picasso's work. Moving from period to period, visitors can easily grasp the relationships among his works and watch themes and styles develop. From these insights grows a deeper and clearer understanding of Picasso's great and unique contributions to the world of art.

Just as the map in the Picasso museum shows how the museum is organized, an organizational structure that a reader can easily follow sets the first standard for a portfolio. The standard is organization—each student's portfolio has labeled sections arranged in a logical and easily used sequence.

PRIMARY EXAMPLE

Targeted Intelligences: Logical/Mathematical, Verbal/Linguistic

Targeted Standard: Problem solving and accuracy

Section A: Problem solving (chronological order)
1. Student goal card for selected intelligence
2. Teacher check list of observed problem solving in group
3. Student self-check list for problem-solving step use
4. Student-selected samples of accuracy in math problem solving (2)
5. Student-selected samples of personal problem solving (2)

Section B: Accuracy
1. Student goal card for selected intelligence
2. Student-selected samples of accurate work in computation (3)
3. Student-selected samples of accurate written work (3)
4. Teacher note about homework

MIDDLE GRADE EXAMPLE

Targeted Intelligences: All
Targeted Standard: Problem Solving

Table of Contents and Teacher Check List

Section A: *Visual/Spatial*
1. Map of archeological dig site with article and group PM
2. Photos of group and self in dig
3. Photos of found items in dig
4. Two sketches of dig items found

Section B: *Verbal/Linguistic*
1. Personal KWL about ancient artifacts
2. Poem about trip to dig museum
3. Daily dig journal: focus on problem solving
4. Classroom notes on archeological digs

Section C: *Logical/Mathematical*
1. Measurements of dig site and proportions
2. Calculations of time estimates
3. Teacher check list of observed problem-solving behavior

Section D: *Interpersonal*
1. Group check list of group cooperation and problem solving
2. Group notes on contributions to group problem solving
3. Staff award for "most congenial digger"

Section E: *Intrapersonal*
1. My "learning goals for the dig" list
2. Summary evaluation of project portfolio: How we solved our dig problems

Section F: *Musical/Rhythmic*
1. Group song from dig banquet and awards night
2. Sketch of musical instruments from culture

Section G: *Bodily/Kinesthetic*
1. Photo of self digging with pick and ax
2. Group photo of dance replicating culture's ceremonial dance

Section H: *Naturalist*
1. Classification of artifacts.
2. Report on observations of similar attributes of fossils.

SECONDARY EXAMPLE: A UNIT FROM U.S. GOVERNMENT COURSE

Targeted Intelligences: Visual/Spatial, Verbal/Linguistic
Targeted Standard: Complex Thinking—Each student will show the relationships among the branches of national government in resolving a domestic issue of national significance.

Table of Contents and Evaluation Comment Sheet

	Date	A	B	C	D	Comments
Section A: *The Executive Branch*						
1. Research cards						
2. Diagram of responsibilities						
3. Description of role in dispute						
Section B: *The Judicial Branch*						
1. Research cards						
2. Diagram of responsibilities						
3. Description of role in dispute						
Section C: *The Legislative Branch*						
1. Research cards						
2. Diagram of responsibilities						
3. Description of role in dispute						
Section D: *The Connections*						
1. Tree map						
2. Teacher-made final exam						

TECH PREP EXAMPLE: GRAPHIC DESIGN COURSE PORTFOLIO

Targeted Intelligence: Visual/Spatial
Targeted Standard: Precision—The student will use principles of design in building a model home.

Table of Contents and Evaluation Check Sheet

RUBRIC

	A	B	C	D	F	Comments
Section 1: *Design Work*						
a. Rough sketches and consumer feedback chart						
b. Final floor plan						
c. List of needed materials						
Section 2: *Supporting Evidence*						
a. Summary of real estate interviews						
b. Photo album of model house under construction						
c. Daily journal						
d. Award ribbon and certificate						
e. Architect evaluations						

A very helpful aide to organization is the table of contents check list. This serves as the student's organizing guide, a quick check list for the teacher, and if grades are needed, a report card.

TABLE OF CONTENTS EXAMPLE

Name: <u>Vicki Burger</u>   Grade: <u>7</u>

Items in Order	**Completed**	**Points Awarded**
Section I		
1. The Rubric	X	4
2. Journal	X	4
3. Social Studies Concept Map	X	3
4. Short Story	X	2
5. Diorama	X	5
6. Base Group Evaluation	X	3
7. Math Work Sheets	X	4
8. Semester Knowledge Test	X	3
		——
	Total	28
	Score	3.5
	Grade	C+

Make Your Own

TARGETED INTELLIGENCE:

TARGETED STANDARD:

TABLE OF CONTENTS:

········ THE RUBRIC ········

Standard:

Criteria	1	2	3	4

Tools:

Comments:

_____

_____

_____

Final Grade: _____

Scale
_____ = A
_____ = B
_____ = C
Below ___ = Not Yet

Selective

The second standard for a well-constructed portfolio is selectivity. The selective portfolio is neither a total collection nor a random collection of work. The process of portfolio making requires the student to *select* examples of his or her work that meet the given rubric's standards, criteria, and indicators of success. Sometimes the selection method includes identifying only exemplary or "the best" artifacts. At other times, the selection method may identify the "best," "good," and "not-so-good" examples.

The selection standards and criteria must reflect the seriousness of the learning process. The portfolio is neither a game nor "busy work." If it is used for these purposes, it would be better not to use it at all.

For students to take the portfolio seriously, they must learn to take the responsibility for selecting what is the best of their academic work. Contrast these good and bad examples of portfolio use according to a *selection* scale.

PRIMARY EXAMPLES

An example of unacceptable portfolio use

Each nine weeks, teachers in the Smithton Elementary School invite the children to decorate empty grocery boxes. One day a week, each student is given a box and one hour to decorate it. At the end of the week, the teacher selects one piece of work for the student to date and put into the box. One week, the entry may be a math work sheet; another week, a self-concept activity sheet. Discipline slips are also included.

The principal created the random system as a way to "to raise the children's anxiety" about their daily work and behavior. "They know the box goes home, but they can never guess what will be in it before the teacher picks. When the parents see the box, they get a picture of what the child has done that week."

|--|--**X**

Promotes   Allows   Not Yet
Student   Student
Selectivity   Selection

An example of acceptable portfolio use

At the beginning of the school year, teachers at Thomasville Elementary construct a "Guidelines for Your Most Intelligent Work" chart. The students in each class brainstorm lists of indicators of most intelligent work for each of the multiple intelligences. The lists are posted, and each teacher assists the students in preparing the first quarter's goals in the targeted intelligence. Each student writes his or her name on a manila folder and makes symbols to represent three selected goals. Inside the folder, the student puts one symbol in each of three colored dividers. At the end of each week, the

---

student selects one artifact of classroom work that he or she thinks represents "my most intelligent work" for each of the three goals. On Fridays, children sit in the "I-am-smart chair" and share their selections with the class. At the end of the quarter, each student selects "my most intelligent work." The teacher sends the selected work home with the report card.

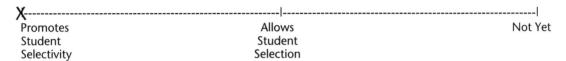

Promotes	Allows	Not Yet
Student	Student	
Selectivity	Selection	

SECONDARY EXAMPLES

An example of unacceptable portfolio use

In the first week of September, all freshmen are assigned into a counseling group with 250 peers and a counselor. Each receives the following letter from the principal.

```
Dear Student:

  Welcome to New Rapids High School. In the four short years that you will be
here, you will want to collect valuable memories of your high school years. As
part of your graduation requirement, you must assemble a collection of those
memories. We call this your graduation portfolio. By our state law, you cannot
graduate without this portfolio.

  What you put in the portfolio is up to you. Consider it to be your private
yearbook. In past years, students have included pictures of their friends and
family, mementos of social events, athletic letters and pins, report cards, and
the like.

  Sincerely,

  Benjamin Thorson
```

Promotes	Allows	Not Yet
Student	Student	
Selectivity	Selection	

An example of acceptable portfolio use

In the first week of September, all freshmen are introduced to the Centerville High School graduation requirements. This includes a discussion of the grading method for each class with the performance standards that the teacher will use and the creation of a yearly portfolio. In each class, the teacher describes the method the students will use to select samples of their best academic work for the portfolio. For instance, in English classes, the students will select the best test each wrote, the best essay or creative writing piece, and the best journal entry. At the end of each year, their counselor collects the portfolios. At the end of the first semester of the senior year, each senior prepares an overview of his or her three best samples from all classes up to this time and explains why each was selected. In addition, the student proposes a graduation project for the final semester. A faculty committee reviews each portfolio, each plan, and each student's course transcript. Students whose plans are approved may earn a semester's credit for completing and evaluating the senior project.

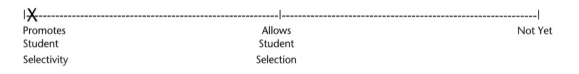

Promotes	Allows	Not Yet
Student	Student	
Selectivity	Selection	

On the selectivity scale, the unacceptable examples should be marked "not yet." First, the unacceptable assessment systems put more emphasis on the teacher's selection than on the students'. If the teachers do the selecting, the students never have the chance to learn through success and failure. The students can go through the motions of putting together a portfolio, but a portfolio that has no significance for them. Second, in both cases, the standards and the criteria for assessment of the portfolio are random and fuzzy. The students are expected to guess their way. While some may guess well and create a meaningful portfolio, history shows that most of their work will be perfunctory.

On the other hand, the acceptable examples show that the teachers are serious about portfolios filled with work that helps students make sound choices. The teachers provide clear instructions and examples. They also give the students ample opportunity to experience success by learning how to assess the best work they do.

Promoting selectivity is best accomplished when the teacher and parents work together to teach students how to select for the portfolio in a "learn-by-doing" mode. In a Georgia elementary school, the leadership team determined that accuracy, problem solving, and transfer of learning would be the exit standards for the eighth grade. Each teacher posted the standards, grade-level criteria, and indicators on the class bulletin board. Each teacher sent the parents a letter that discussed how he or she would use the rubric that year. In explaining "why," each teacher targeted two or three intelligences for special attention in the year's work. The primary teachers spoke about their special emphasis on language development through multiple means of written, oral, and visual tasks. They connected this to an explanation of the importance of developing the verbal/linguistic and visual/spatial intelligences for children of this age.

The middle grade teachers selected a project-based learning approach. Before beginning a project, students in cooperative groups reviewed the three exit standards and developed their own indicators for assessing the project. Each group wrote a letter to the parents. The letters outlined what project the group was doing, why they selected the project, and how they and

MIDDLE GRADE EXAMPLES

I	II	III
What Construct ?	A model of Fort Oglethorpe	Build an energy flow machine
Research:	Books on the history of Georgia	Library articles on energy flow
Standard:	Accuracy	Problem solving
Criteria:	Know facts about building this fort Make a detailed plan Build a precise model to scale	Know theory of energy flow Do math calculations Build machine from scrap materials
Indicators:	90% on history quiz Essay on famous person Sketch matches detailed plans in text Scale of fort Connect each object to accuracy	Explain how machine flows energy Vocabulary test at 95% Correct calculations at 100% Machine works Describe problem-solving steps
Intelligences:	Visual/spatial Interpersonal Verbal/linguistic Logical/mathematical	Logical/mathematical Verbal/linguistic Interpersonal Visual/spatial
Time:	14 hours	9 hours

Assessment: Parent review of accuracy. Demonstration to parents with check lists given to teacher.

their parents would evaluate the final work according to the three standards of accuracy, problem solving, and transfer of learning. Note how each of these two groups designed a different project but managed to include a collaborative assessment by students and parents.

Representative

The third standard for a well-constructed portfolio, representativeness, gives balance to the selectivity standard. While the selectivity standard enables students to learn how to make meaningful choices about the quality of their work (within guidelines set by the school community), the *representativeness* standard highlights individual development of the intelligences and internal motivation.

A portfolio that is representative provides a *multidimensional* picture of the student's many intelligences. It contains examples of a student's work not only with the traditional emphasis on logical/mathematical and verbal/linguistic work, but also with his or her visual/spatial, musical/rhythmic, interpersonal, intrapersonal, naturalist, and bodily/kinesthetic achievements and potentials. Moreover, the representative portfolio contains assessments of this wider range of work from multiple perspectives. These perspectives may include assessments by the student, his or her peers, other adults, the teacher, and his or her parents.

From the earliest years, the teacher mediates the student's selection of contents for the portfolio. As the student learns how to organize the portfolio and then select "best works," he or she also learns to make sure the portfolio has a balance of materials. The multiple intelligences provide an ideal framework for inviting the student to investigate the widest range of possible abilities. The framework prevents the student from retreating into a narrow and limited "doing what I like to do." With the representative standard, the teacher can challenge the student to move out of comfort zones and into discomfort zones. Following the pathway to maximum development of an intelligence, the teacher can encourage the student to travel from the "encounter" stage to the "embrace" stage in as many of the intelligences as possible.

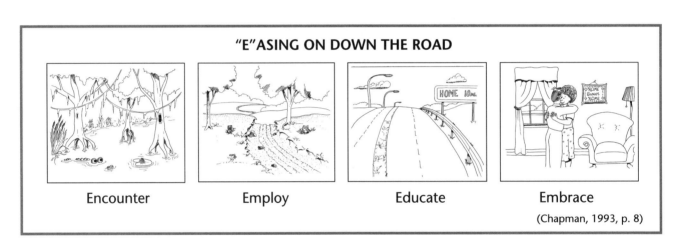

"E"ASING ON DOWN THE ROAD

Encounter   Employ   Educate   Embrace

(Chapman, 1993, p. 8)

By organizing the exit portfolio according to the multiple intelligences, each student can include a journey assessment sheet similar to the examples adapted from *If the Shoe Fits...: How to Develop Multiple Intelligences in the Classroom* (Chapman, 1993, p 8). With the rubrics completed, the teacher and the student may make periodic entries to assess progress over many semesters along the way. By making the journey rubric the divider in the portfolio, each year the teacher, parent, and student can review the student's progress and refer to "best work" artifacts collected each year for each intelligence.

Each year brings a new representative assessment of the student's performances. In the final year, the teacher facilitates a final portrait. This portrait highlights the student's strengths and potential in many dimensions.

PERSONAL STRENGTH SUMMARY

Name_____   Class_____

Intelligences	Reasons	Comments
_____	_____	_____
_____	_____	_____
_____	_____	_____
_____	_____	_____
_____	_____	_____

Promotes insight

The final important standard for a well-constructed portfolio is that it *promotes insight*. It is easy to make a portfolio that collects artifacts of activities. It is difficult to select artifacts that facilitate self-knowledge. Educators have continually struggled to find ways to encourage students to learn, to reflect, and to apply their learning to their lives. In today's classrooms many students believe it is the teacher's job to impart information, to motivate, and to entertain. Teachers who attempt to mediate reflective thinking and facilitate the students' search for meaning know from experience that they will meet resistance.

The portfolio that meets the organization, selectivity, and representative standards to a high degree is an important starting point for promoting student insight into the development of his or her many intelligences.

With the rubrics and the artifacts at his or her disposal, the teacher as *cognitive mediator* has a variety of tools for helping students to examine the connecting threads, the challenges, and the promise found in their portfolios.

PRIMARY EXAMPLES

Mirror, Mirror on the Wall

This reflection strategy works well with cooperative groups. Each child receives a copy of the mirror blackline. In turn, each shares his or her best work in each of the intelligences. (As a prompt, the bulletin board names each of the intelligences and shows pictures of people using each.) The other members of the group help the focus child pick out the three best examples for that child. The group helps the child sketch a symbol for each of the three on the mirror blackline. When all are finished, the teacher provides the

children with a note to take home. He or she role-plays what will happen when the child shows the mirror to his or her parent(s) and tells about the examples on his or her mirror.

KWL—An Adaptation from Donna Ogle's Prereading Strategy (Ogle, 1986)

K	W	L

All children are given a copy of the KWL chart. In the K column, the teacher asks them to write what they "know" about their intelligences, and in the W column, what they "want" to improve in their intelligences. The teacher next helps the children select the most important "want" and make that a goal for the next grading period. The chart is put into the portfolio until the end of the grading period. At this time, the children fill in the "learned" (L) column to tell what they learned about their intelligences.

Footsteps

Before starting a new lesson in a targeted intelligence, the teacher helps the students cut out three to five footprints. On the reverse side of each cutout, the student writes his or her name. The teacher tells the students that after the project is finished, the class will brainstorm all the things people did well in completing the task. Then each student will select what he or she did well and write one example on each footprint. After signing his or her footprints, each student tacks them on the "easing down the road to intelligence" bulletin board.

MIDDLE GRADES EXAMPLES

Snapshot Sequence

At the end of the marking period, the teacher gives each student twelve to eighteen index cards. Each student selects his or her strongest intelligence. Reviewing the artifacts in the portfolio, the student writes words or draws images that represent how he or she has "walked the road" for this intelligence. As cues, the teacher can use an overhead to show the generic road, and the students can refer to the rubrics and their artifacts to help sequence the cards from "encounter" to "embrace." The students can name their roads and glue the cards to poster board for display. Finally, the teacher may invite several students to explain their snapshot sequences before each places it into his or her portfolio.

Video Interview

At the end of a year, students select those items from their portfolios that represent their best development in each intelligence. Next, they will use a ranking ladder to rank-order their level of development among the intelligences. They then prepare a reason for each of the placements. When ready, they participate with a team in an interview. In round robin style, each team member (a) works the camera, (b) interviews, and (c) is interviewed. The team may imitate any television interview show. The interviewer asks: "What intelligence did you most improve this year?" "Why do you think so?" He or she repeats the questions for the three top-ranked intelligences. The interviewee may show artifacts, the rank ladder, etc. Each interview concludes with the question: "And which intelligence do you want to most improve?" After the students take their videos home and share them with their families, they place them in their respective portfolios.

On Target

At the end of a project, each student labels the central circle of the target with the name of the target intelligences. Other intelligences are featured in the outer circles. Under or near each label, the student gives a number rating (1= low, 5= high) to indicate how well he or she did in using this intelligence in the project. On lines at the bottom, the student lists reasons for his or her central choice before placing the target in the portfolio.

Reasons: _____
_____
_____
_____
_____

SECONDARY EXAMPLES

Bar Graph/Pair Share

At the end of a marking period, each student reviews his or her portfolio for the course. The teacher provides a blank bar graph. Each student lists the intelligences he or she targeted for improvement in the marking period and graphs the amount of improvement achieved. At the bottom of the graph, he or she indicates reasons for the intelligence with the most improvement. After the graph is done, each student pairs with a partner and shares the graph and reasons before putting the graph in the portfolio.

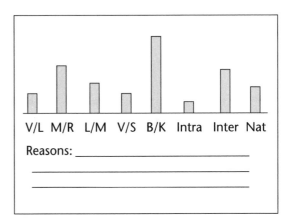

V/L M/R L/M V/S B/K Intra Inter Nat

Reasons: _____
_____
_____

Goal Review

Before starting a lesson, unit, or project, the teacher asks each student to select one intelligence that he or she wishes to develop. On an index card or in his or her journal, the student lists reasons for this selection. After all have completed their notes, the teacher pairs each student with a partner.

Each person in the pair takes turns asking the following sequence of questions shown on the overhead or in a handout:

What is the intelligence you selected?
Why did you decide to work on this intelligence?
What will be your standard?
How will you know that you are making the improvements your want?

At the end of the lesson, the same pairs get together to discuss these questions:
What was the intelligence you selected?
What was your goal?
What did you do well in reaching that goal?
What would you do differently if given the same chance again?
How pleased are you with what you accomplished?

At the conclusion of the interview, each student uses a note card or journal to summarize what was accomplished with the intelligence goal. The pairs may share the summaries before placing them in the portfolio.

Check List

After reviewing the rubric for a lesson or project, the teacher gives each student a blank copy of the check list. Each enters five indicators for the project standard on the check list. Midway through the unit, each student checks progress made to that date. At the end of the lesson, each student checks and dates the final assessment.

If using the check list for an entire marking period, the students enter standards on it. At three-week intervals, the students review progress, date the entries, and return the check list to the portfolio.

Name_____ Date_____
Intelligence_____ Goal_____

                                                    Date
1._____ _____
2._____ _____
3._____ _____
4._____ _____
5._____ _____

To assist students with judgments about their own work and development, it is best for the teacher to go beyond the facilitating role. The facilitating teacher supplies assessment formats similar to the preceding examples and gives instructions, models, and encouragement to the students. Beyond the facilitating role is the mediating role (Feuerstein et al., 1985; Fogarty, 1994.) The mediating teacher gives the students the opportunity to talk aloud about their judgments and to help them think more clearly about the specifics of their assessments. The mediator does not lecture, make comments, encourage, discourage, or react to the student's thoughts. The mediator asks precise questions that challenge the student to think more clearly about his or her own judgments.

Mediating questions work best in a climate where students listen to each other, respect individual responses, and avoid making verbal or nonverbal comments that would discourage another student's public expression of ideas. They also work best when the teacher-mediator explains to the students what he or she is doing and why for each mediating question and how he or she will wait for the responses. Some of the questions or phrases that help mediate a student's insight are open-ended and invitational in tone.

EXAMPLES OF MEDIATING QUESTIONS

1. I would appreciate it if you could tell us what you did in this project.

2. I would like you to tell us why you selected. . . .

3. I wonder what else you might have to say about. . . .

4. I am not clear about what you mean by. . . . Could you give me an example?

5. You sound (feeling) about_____? Am I right?

6. Why do you think_____?

7. How pleased are you about_____?

8. What pleases you most about_____?

9. How would you do it differently?

10. What help do you need?

In most instances, these launch questions ask the student to describe what he or she did. After that, the mediator seeks to extend the student's thoughts, to clarify, and to facilitate analysis and synthesis by asking the most appropriate, noninterrupting follow-up questions for the situation. At the end of the mediation, the mediator reviews the questions asked.

The mediation role is appropriate for helping even the youngest students gain insight. Through skillful questions, students are helped to reflect on how they learned and how to apply what they learned to other situations.

MEDIATING QUESTIONS IN ACTION

In Mary Nelson's second grade class, the students used the logical/mathematical strategy for estimating the number of blocks in a wall they would construct (see page 100). After the measurements were recorded by the groups, Mary gathered all the groups around her rocking chair. First, she praised them for the intensity of their cooperative problem solving. Next, she told them that they were going to review what they had done and the thinking that the task took.

"First I want us to remember our rules for 'think aloud' time." Mary said.

Many hands poked the air. "Francisco, what is one rule?"

"Listen to each other," answered Francisco.

"Sue Ellen?"

"Don't make fun or laugh," said the tiny redhead.

"And George, what will you add?"

George looked blank, "I forgot."

"That's all right, George. Maria?" asked Ms. Nelson softly.

"Don't interrupt."

"That's fine, Maria. And what do you think that big word 'interrupt' means?"

Maria was silent. Ms. Nelson waited. George squirmed.

"It means don't talk when someone else is talking."

"Wonderful, and are there any more ideas?" Mary Nelson looked slowly over her classroom. There were no hands. "Fine," she said. "Let's all remember those rules."

Tommy's hand shot up. "Can I go to the bathroom?"

"Yes," the teacher said. "You may go at any time during the discussion without asking. Just remember to move without distracting us."

Tommy scooted away.

"Now, let's go to my questions about your projects. I don't want to know your answers yet. But I will. I first want to ask the reporter from each group to tell me how you solved the problem."

Tim volunteered. "We all did our jobs. First, we measured our blocks to see how big they were. Then Tommy and Beth measured the room. After that, we took one block and a ruler. We moved the block and counted how many times we moved it. The last thing we did was multiply by three."

Ms. Nelson called on three more groups to describe how they had solved the problem. After she determined there were no new variations, she asked the calculator in each group to tell the class what was the hardest part of the task. This question was followed by a question asking the recorder to tell what was learned about problem solving. When several students struggled, Ms. Nelson coached them. Finally, she came to the application question. "Who is going to tell me how this problem solving will help you learn mathematics?"

Having returned from the bathroom, Tommy raised his hand. "I can help my dad. He is a carpenter."

Ms. Nelson waited a minute. Tommy was silent. "How will this math help you?" she asked.

"Because he has to measure. Sometimes he can't measure. He has to estimate like we did."

"And how are you as an estimator, Tommy."

"I did a good job."

"How so?" asked Ms. Nelson.

"We estimated how many blocks we would need for the wall. After that, we measured the room again. I bet our answer is just right."

While it is important that the student organize a portfolio to select representative work, it is as important that the collection provide insight into his or her learning styles in the various intelligences, his or her strengths and weaknesses, and his or her learning potential. Each section of the portfolio should include an ample representation of self-assessments to go along with teacher observations and check lists.

In the yearly portfolio, the balance created by the collection of the observations of others, the assessments of best performances, and the self-reflections paints a rich multidimensional portrait, a portrait of the student as a young learner with multiple intelligences.

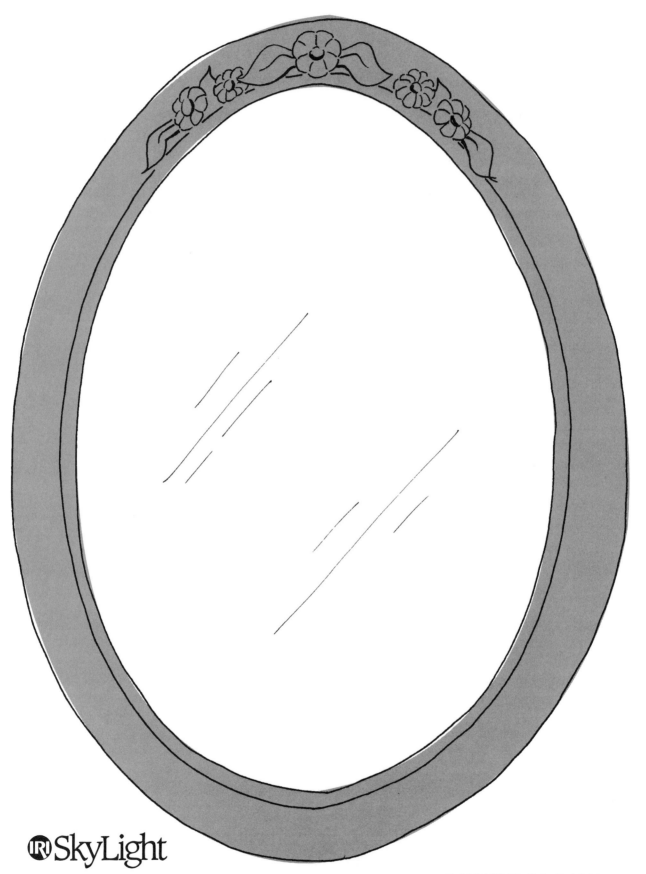

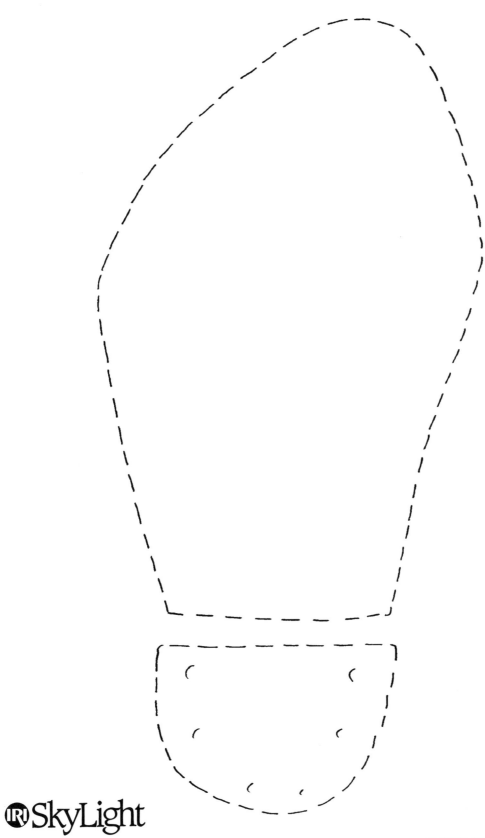

IRI SkyLight

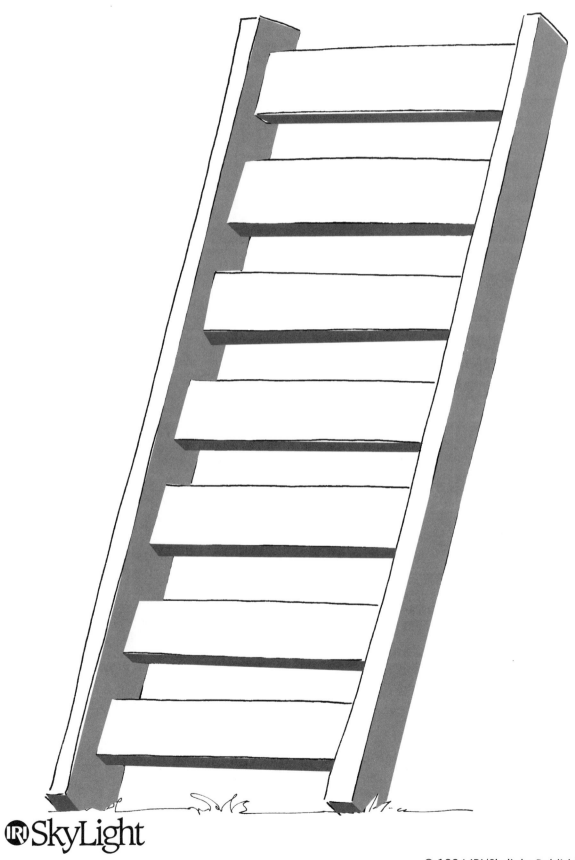

Reasons: _____

_____

_____

_____

_____

_____

_____

13

Communicating Multiple Intelligences Assessment With Parents

Dear Ms. Trueblood:

Welcome to the sixth grade. I am Michael Angelo and I will be Jerry's teacher.

I am writing this letter to give you and Jerry an introduction to a very exciting year. As you may have heard, my classroom is very different from what Jerry may have known in the past years. My classroom is organized to give Jerry and his classmates every chance to be successful. I have organized my classroom around eight learning centers. Each of these centers will help Jerry develop a different talent.

Every child has many talents. To develop these talents, which I call the many intelligences, the student needs my help. But the student has to do the work. Jerry will have to think and be responsible for his learning.

You may be concerned about what he will learn. Be assured that Jerry will learn math and logic, art, music, P.E., reading, and writing just as in past years. He will also learn how to cooperate and work in a team, and he will learn how to evaluate his own work.

Jerry will make a collection of everything he learns. Every four weeks, he will bring home a videotape. On the videotape, he will explain his work, and he will tell you how well or poorly he has been doing. He will also bring home a folder with samples of his work. I hope you will be able to look carefully at his work and answer a questionnaire for me each time.

If you are concerned about his work and want to talk with me, please send a note or call me at the school. I will be happy to discuss your worry or have a conference with you and Jerry.

Sincerely,

Michael Angelo

Ms. Trueblood was not surprised by the letter. Her neighbors, the Johnsons, had a son in Mr. Angelo's class two years ago. She had heard from them about all the different things that happened in the class. She had also heard how unhappy Todd Johnson was when the year was over and he had to move to the seventh grade. The Johnsons had told her how happy they were with the video conferences that Mr. Angelo's students created. Ms. Trueblood was looking forward to the video and the folder of work. Because both parents worked, it was almost impossible for them to get to the annual parent night conferences. She worried about her son at school, and wanted any information she could get.

Mr. Angelo's home video conferences fit right in with his use of the multiple intelligences centers (see Chapman, 1994, p. 39-40 for a full explanation of these centers and how they work in the classroom). Every four weeks, his students select two multiple intelligences centers. Order of choice was determined in a random drawing the week before the shift. Each morning and each afternoon ended with forty minutes of center time. As students worked on center projects, they devised their own rubrics and planned their projects, problem-solving tasks, exhibits, performances, and demonstrations. They also picked how they wanted the work evaluated. Each student had a cardboard valise divided into two parts. One part was for the AM center, the other for the PM center.

At the beginning of the fourth week, teams of three were picked. Each afternoon, the camera equipment (Mr. Angelo's parent group had bought two sets over the years) was rotated among the teams. Each team prepared itself off-camera so that each student could have five to seven minutes to present his or her work on camera. Each student in the class had his or her own videotape. Any parents who wanted to keep a copy had to make their own, because the school videotape was used all year.

Twice a year, Mr. Angelo added his own segment to each student's video. In this segment, he showed clips of the child at work, talked about the highlights of the student's work, and identified areas of concern. Whenever he shared a concern, he also made some suggestions.

The videotapes always went home with the portfolio. After showing the portfolio, the student showed the video and then asked his or her parent(s) to answer Mr. Angelo's questionnaire.

Some parents made a video response to the questions.

Dear Ms. Trueblood:

You have just reviewed Jerry's report card, his collection of work which has my comments on the front page, and his video. It would help me and Jerry if you would respond to these questions. It will give Jerry practice in his interview assignment if you would let him ask the questions and record the answers.

Because we have only one tape per child, it is important that you return Jerry's tape. At the end of the year, you may keep the tape.

Please call me if you have special concerns to discuss.

Sincerely,

Michael Angelo

Student name _____

Parent name(s) _____

Phone _____ Date _____

1. What did you like best about the work Jerry showed to you?

_____

_____

2. What did you like best about what Jerry said on his video about his work?

_____

_____

3. What would you like Jerry to learn more about or do better?

_____

_____

4. I am pleased with Jerry's school work.

----

 very pleased   pleased   not pleased

Comment:

_____

_____

Please call me to discuss this report. ___

I don't need a report. ___

I would like a conference. ___

Parent Signature _____ Date_____

While this very personal video conference has proven to be an exciting tool for communicating with parents and showing the different ways the students can learn in the multiple intelligences classroom, it is not the only way. Note these alternatives.

Audio exchange

Each student receives a set of four, thirty-minute audiotapes. At the end of each quarter, student teams work together to interview each other and the teacher in twenty-minute segments. Each student takes his or her tape home along with his or her portfolio. The parents have a week to review the audiotape and the portfolio and to make a ten-minute response on the audiotape.

Graded portfolio

In districts that require grades as well as the portfolio, the teacher compiles the district's standard report card. To prepare for this, all student tasks end with a point-scaled rubric. Points are tabulated on a grading scale for each heading on the report card. The report card and the portfolio are sent home.

PRIMARY EXAMPLE

Dear Parent:

I am pleased to have your child in the third grade class at Heartland. As you know, each nine weeks, you will receive a report card and a packet of your child's best work. Your child has collected this work and wants you to see it.

If you are wondering how your child received each grade, let me explain our point system. On each of the projects in the packet, you will see a note attached. It looks like this:

NAME: <u>Kay Bethso</u>   DATE: <u>1/23</u>   GRADE: <u>3</u>

Project: Make a book

What I did: I wrote a story. I made the pictures. I glued the pages into a book.

How I did:

My Story Order

Wow	O.K.	Not Yet
	X	
5	3	0

My Story Interest

Wow	O.K.	Not Yet
	—✗—	
5	3	0

My Pictures

Wow	O.K.	Not Yet
✗—		
5	3	0

Comments: *I loved your choice of color. So bright!*

My Binding

Wow	O.K.	Not Yet
		—✗
5	3	0

My Cover Design

Wow	O.K.	Not Yet
	—✗—	
5	3	0

Catches the Eye

Wow	O.K.	Not Yet
✗—		
5	3	0

Total Score: 19

I turn student points into the grades on the report card. There are 100 points each quarter in each subject. This is my grading scale:

90+ = A
85+ = B
80+ = C
75+ = D

Each student has this scale in his or her portfolio. Each week, your child can tell you the point total.

The portfolio is for you to look over with your child. You may keep it at home. If you need to contact me, please call the school office.

Sincerely,

Ms. Yvette Major

REPORT CARD

HEARTLAND ELEMENTARY SCHOOL

NAME: <u>Sylvia Jones</u>   YEAR: <u>1995-6</u>   TEACHER: <u>Ms. Major</u>

Subject	Quarter				Final Comment
Quarter	1	2	3	4	
Reading	A	B	A-		
Mathematics	C	B	B		
Science	B	B	B+		
History	A	A	A		Great work
Writing	B	B	B		
Spelling	C	D	C		Needs to study
Attendance	0	2	0		
Behavior	A	B	B		

Parent Signature

1. _____

2. _____

3. _____

MIDDLE GRADES EXAMPLE

DUSABLE MIDDLE SCHOOL REPORT CART

NAME: <u>Richardo Menendez</u>   GRADE: <u>7</u>   ADVISOR: <u>Mr. Mestopolis</u>

| Intelligence | Marking Period | | | | Comments |
	1	2	3	4	
Verbal/Linguistic	91	97			
Visual/Spatial	62	75			
Musical/Rhythmic	68	68			
Bodily/Kinesthetic	94	96			
Interpersonal	93	98			A leader
Logical/Mathematical	85	81			
Intrapersonal	61	65			A doer
Naturalist	81	95			

Dear Parent:

With your child's report card, you have received his or her portfolio. When you read the portfolio, you will get a more detailed idea about the quarter's number grade.

Since we do not pass these grades on to the high school, these numbers are meant only to give you a picture of his or her relative strengths and weaknesses in each of the intelligences.

As you learned on the first parent night, we are working to give your child a balanced education. It is very unusual for a child to do equally well in all areas. For each of the intelligences, we use this scale:

High performer:	90+
Strong performer:	80+
Adequate performer:	70+
Passing performer:	60+

These are not competitive grades. Performance points are earned in a variety of ways. If you are concerned about your child's performance in any of the areas, please call his or her advisor here at school.

Sincerely
Beth Kay, Ph.D.
Principal

SECONDARY EXAMPLE

BELVIDERE HIGH SCHOOL COURSE REPORT

NAME: <u>Maureen Conick</u>   COURSE: <u>Interdisciplinary Studies</u>

TEACHER: <u>James O'Bell</u>

Standard	Marking Period				Comments
	1	2	3	4	
Problem solving	24				Explores ideas well
Connections	17				Not tying ideas together
Precision	25				
Completeness	<u>13</u>				Need to carry out with example
Total	79				

grade scale 93+ = A, 85+ = B, 78+ = C, 70+ = D

Video yearbook

Each week, a new team of three to five students becomes the video recording team. The team is assigned one intelligence on which it will focus the camera.

With the teacher's assistance, the team plans who and what it will shoot in the classroom. Each day, the team devotes one hour to gathering its footage. On Friday, the team works at the computer to edit the best footage for inclusion in the class yearbook. Once a quarter, the class votes on the best footage in each intelligence. For the next quarter, the teams change. In the last quarter, seven new teams, each assigned an intelligence, do the final editing for that intelligence. Finally, all the tape is sequenced and duplicated so that each student has a copy of the class video yearbook.

Computer processfolio

Howard Gardner is a strong advocate of processfolios, which make problem-solving the focus of the assessment. The computer is well-equipped for such a task. To create a computer-based folio, the teacher needs a small scanner, a computer, and a laser printer in the classroom. The teacher makes a master diskette organized to collect student data, copy artifacts or pictures of artifacts, and write reports. Students will have the opportunity to scan reports and photos of artifacts into the sections of the processfolio that the teacher has organized like any other port-folio. After the students scan in their completed work, the program allows both the teacher and the student to use Likert scales, check lists, and comments to assess the quality of the students' work. At the end of the marking period, the program may have the capacity to total points and assign a grade or print out select portions or all of the student's work.

Student-led conference

Students and teachers prepare portfolios and schedule conferences during which the students discuss their portfolios with their parents. The teacher has the option of scheduling several conferences in the same room at the same time so that the students are the focal point, not the teacher or parent. The student and parent sit and discuss the portfolio; the student conducts the conference and shares what he or she is learning. It is a very positive experience for parents and students. The teacher moves from conference to conference and joins in briefly. In this way, the teacher is available, as needed. Teachers who set up conferences like this are always pleased with the way students can discuss what they are learning, what they are working on, and how they feel about their experiences. So many times this is an eye opener for parents, because they realize just how much their children are learning and applying their learning to other areas.

**STUDENT-PARENT CONFERENCE
PLANNING OUTLINE**

Name:_____Grade:_____Conference Date:_____

1. What are the best (most important, most liked, most pleasing) examples of your work that you want to share with your parent(s). Be sure to pick from each of your intelligences.

2. Tell how your work fits the class performance standards.

3. Plan a start for your conference.

4. Plan an ending for your conference.

STUDENT-PARENT CONFERENCE
PARENT REACTION

Name of Student: _____ Date: _____

Parent Name: _____

What I learned from this conference. _____

_____

What pleased me about this conference. _____

_____

What concerned me about this conference. _____

_____

Signatures:

_____

☐ Please call me to discuss the conference.

Conclusion

At a time when educators and the community seek better ways to prepare all students for living, learning, and working in the emerging high-tech, information-rich world of the twenty-first century, Gardner's theory of multiple intelligences provides classroom teachers and school reformers with a new perspective. The multiple intelligences perspective opens the door to many exciting and challenging new ways for learning to occur. The theory shows teachers the opportunities to use new methods, processes, and strategies.

However, it is still imperative for teachers to remember the importance of the balanced Tyler triangle. More than half a century ago, Ralph Tyler clearly demonstrated the interconnectedness of instruction, curriculum, and assessment. Changing one side of the triangle without changing the other two can only end in loss of critical balance. Thus, as teachers investigate new instructional strategies and processes to fit the Gardner theory, they cannot forget to seek out corresponding changes in curriculum and assessment. Keeping the three sides equal is a challenge.

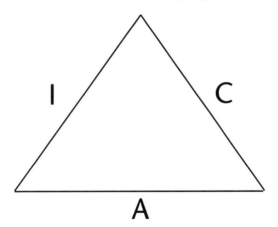

In this book, you have focused on how to change assessment to match changes in instructional approaches aligned with the theory of multiple intelligences. Throughout the chapters, you have examined a variety of standards for measuring each intelligence and have framed rubrics that you can use with multiple intelligences-based lessons. You used model lessons from *If the Shoe Fits…: How to Develop Multiple Intelligences in the Classroom* (Chapman, 1993) to guide the creation of your own rubrics. The authors kept the assessment examples close to the content found in most classrooms. This will make it easier for you to develop assessments within your curriculum, but from a multiple intelligences perspective. But remember, the more you change your instructional and assessment strategies in the light of Gardner's theory, the more you should reexamine the curriculum.

If the curriculum you are now teaching is mired in lower-level outcomes filled with mastery of factual information and isolated basic skills, you can improve it with many of the motivational strategies associated with the multiple intelligences. Your students cannot help but benefit from the variety and interest that these strategies will bring to the classroom.

As soon as you combine authentic assessments with multiple intelligences strategies, you will present your students with the opportunity to meet high performance standards. You can switch the students' attention from mastery of facts and figures to a deeper understanding of the processes of learning. The facts and figures will follow, but they will no longer drive what and how you teach.

A process-driven curriculum built on the theory of multiple intelligences is not incompatible with the standardized tests that many states and districts mandate. Students will still master those basic facts and figures, not for a test, but as tools for solving problems, completing complex projects, and exploring new dimensions of learning. All of these tool are assessable with the authentic tools you have examined in this book.

To speed the development of a curriculum fully compatible with multiple intelligences theory, you may find it easier to begin with problem-based learning. Problem-based learning starts with the assumption that students may know little about a particular problem, but through the use of their intelligences, they can solve the problem. Consider these examples:

Content Area: Social Studies
Lesson: Washington at Valley Forge

	Traditional Approach	**Interim Approach**	**Problem-Based Approach**
Instruction	Students read chapter in text.	Students jigsaw text reading in coopera-groups.	Teacher uses KWL to check prior knowledge about Washington's situation at Valley Forge. Students categorize **W** (want to know) list.
	Teacher lectures on topic.	Students explain jigsaw to class.	Student interest groups research selected W and write radio news show on new information. They present the news show.

	Traditional Approach	Interim Approach	Problem-Based Approach
Instruction (cont.)	Teachers show short movie.	Students role-play decisive scenes in groups.	Teacher facilitates "what if?" exploration of different decision points for Washington. Teacher provides rubric for radio plays to follow and for the process of transforming historic facts into creative drama.
	Teacher assigns vocabulary for homework.	Students jigsaw vocabulary and make rap song.	Students use information to carry out "what if?" scenario in radio play. Students enact radio play. After play, students explain and defend rationale.
Assessment	Vocabulary quiz, pop reading quiz, multiple-choice final exam	Teacher gives vocabulary quiz and multiple-choice exam.	Teacher and students use rubric to assess radio play for accuracy of information, logic of rationale, participation, and knowledge of event.
		Students assess group work and write in journals.	

In the problem-based approach, it is not difficult to see how the focus of learning changes from facts and figures to the process of solving "what if?" decision points. With the help of the rubric, the teacher can forget the memory test and spend the time helping students assess their knowledge of the historic event as well as their problem-solving logic. As the students work through their examination of how they solved the problem, they grow rich in the development of their multiple abilities to solve any problem that they are going to face in history classes or in any other domain. In this context, assessment balances well with curricular content and instructional strategy and challenges students to make creative use of their many intelligences.

As the Chinese proverb goes, "Give him a fish and he will eat for a day; teach him to fish and he will eat for a lifetime."

Glossary

Alignment
Arrangement in a straight line; matching (e.g., alignment of curriculum and instructional goals to assessment and evaluation).

Assessment
Judging, valuing, appraising one's work; evaluating.

Authentic Assessment
The evaluation of a student's learning through a broad array of observable evidence (e.g., performance).

Concept
A notion or an idea; a big idea or an overriding, umbrella idea.

Demonstration
A description or explanation of a process; an illustration or example.

Double-Entry Response
Tool used to promote two-way conversations on paper between student and teacher, or between first impression and revisited reflection.

Evaluation
To determine or set value; judgment; critique.

Example
Something selected to show the nature or character of the rest.

Exhibit
To display a product; to show through a public display.

Feedback
A process in which the factors that produce a result are modified, corrected, or strengthened; responses and impressions about something.

Graphic Organizer
Visual format used to organize ideas, concepts, and information; visual organizer or graphic representation (e.g., web, Venn diagram).

Guided Responses

Student responses to questions as directed by a leader or teacher (e.g., a teacher asks students to complete an open-ended statement: My favorite book is . . .).

Indicator

A specific observable behavior that depicts a level of achievement along a continuum or on a scoring rubric.

Journal

A student diary consisting of verbal and visual entries that usually include personal reflections, self-assessments, spontaneous writing, and responses to the learning.

Lesson

A part of a book or an exercise assigned to a student for study.

Likert Scale

Measurement tool that assesses performance on a gradient scale; also used to rate opinions, show a position on an issue, and indicate frequency of occurrence (e.g., 1 = never, 3 = sometimes, 5 = always).

Multiple Intelligences

Verbal/Linguistic Intelligence
The ability to use with clarity the core operations of language.

Musical/Rhythmic Intelligence
The ability to use the core set of musical elements.

Logical/Mathematical Intelligence
The ability to use inductive and deductive reasoning, solve abstract problems, and understand complex relationships.

Interpersonal Intelligence
The ability to get along with, interact with, work with, and motivate others toward a common goal.

Visual/Spatial Intelligence
The ability to perceive the visual world accurately and to be able to recreate one's visual experiences through graphic representations.

Intrapersonal Intelligence
The ability to form an accurate model of oneself and to use that model to operate effectively in life.

Bodily/Kinesthetic Intelligence
The ability to control and interpret body motions, manipulate physical objects, and establish harmony between the body and mind.

Naturalist Intelligence
The ability to see similarities and differences in one's environment and to understand the interrelationships of the ecosystem.

Observation Check List

A strategy to monitor specific skills, behaviors, or dispositions of individual students in the class.

Observation Note Cards

A strategy to monitor specific skills, behaviors, or dispositions of individuals in the class, with notes being kept on cards that are given to the student.

Open-Ended Responses

Divergent, ambiguous, or paradoxical questions and/or responses.

Performance

Any tangible or observable product that students create that allows them to apply and demonstrate what they have learned; hands-on learning; demonstrations.

PMI

Graphic organizer and/or thinking strategy used to identify the pluses, minuses, and interesting (or intriguing) questions related to an activity or lesson (developed by Edward de Bono, 1976).

Portfolios

Selected collection of student work with student reflections that show development and growth; also used to collect a group's or class's work.

Promotes Insight
New ideas and self-knowledge gained as a result of reflection and assessment.

Representative
Highlights individual development through a sampling of the intelligence.

Selective
Meaningful student choices about the student's work or growth and development.

Problem-Solving Process

Analyzing a problem, developing a workable plan or system to solve the problem, then evaluating plan's success.

Product

Something produced by nature or made by humans; an object or program.

Project

A formal, authentic, hands-on assignment given to an individual student or a group of students on a topic related to the curriculum.

Reflection

The result of thoughts, ideas, or conclusions expressed in word; responses to thoughtful interludes.

Rubric

Assessment tool that specifies criteria for different levels of performance; scoring framework or grid that delineates levels and quality of a performance or act.

Standardized Tests

Tests administered and scored under conditions uniform to all students; norm-referenced tests.

Standard

An established rule used to measure quantity and quality; a "yardstick" against which performance is measured, to show the degrees of success and the highest possible level of success.

Content

Any task that requires the use of important knowledge and skill in specific subject areas; knowledge, skills, and concepts related to a field of study.

Performance

A norm established by reliable, authoritative practitioners against which academic performances are measured; a way to determine the quality and quantity of a student's ability to apply knowledge and skills based on established standards.

Process

A procedure in which standards are established, defined, and disseminated for use as an acceptable criterion.

Lifelong

Knowledge and skills that transcend content areas and subject disciplines and that have application for life.

Exit

End goals, aims, and objectives as students "exit" the school system.

Strategy

Plan or procedure for use in various circumstances.

Teacher-Made Tests

Written or oral assessments that are not commercially produced or standardized, but are specifically designed for students by teachers; criterion-referenced tests.

Three-Story Intellect Verbs

Different levels of thinking; e.g., one-story or factual recall, two-story processing, and three-story application. Also called three-level questions.

Tool

An instrument, strategy, or technique for learning.

Bibliography

Bellanca, J. A. (1992). Classroom 2001: Evolution, not revolution. In A. L. Costa, J. A. Bellanca, & R. Fogarty (Eds.), *If minds matter: A foreword to the future, Volume II* (p. 161–165). Arlington Heights, Ill.: IRI/SkyLight Training and Publishing, Inc.

Bellanca, J. A. (1992b). How to grade (if you must). In A. L. Costa, J. A. Bellanca, & R. Fogarty (Eds.), *If minds matter: A foreword to the future, Volume II* (p. 297–311). Arlington Heights, Ill.: IRI/SkyLight Training and Publishing, Inc.

Bellanca, J., & Fogarty, R. (1993). *Catch them thinking.* Arlington Heights, Ill.: IRI/SkyLight Training and Publishing, Inc.

Bellanca, J., & Fogarty, R. (1991). *Blueprints for thinking in the cooperative classroom* (2nd ed.). Arlington Heights, Ill.: IRI/SkyLight Training and Publishing, Inc.

Blythe, T., & Gardner, H. (1990, April). A school for all intelligences. *Educational Leadership, 47*(7), 33–37.

Brandt, R. (1992a, May). On performance assessment: A conversation with Grant Wiggins. *Educational Leadership*, p. 35–37.

Brandt, R. (1992b, May). Overview: A fresh focus for curriculum. *Educational Leadership*, p. 7.

Brownlie, F., Close, S., & Wingren, L. (1990). *Tomorrow's classroom today.* Portsmouth, NH: Heinemann.

Burke, K. A. (1993). *The mindful school: How to assess authentic learning.* Arlington Heights, Ill.: IRI/SkyLight Training and Publishing, Inc.

Burke, K. A. (Ed.) (1992). *Authentic assessment: A collection.* Arlington Heights, Ill.: IRI/SkyLight Training and Publishing, Inc.

Burke, K., Fogarty, R. & Belgrad, S. (1994). *The mindful school: The portfolio connection.* Arlington Heights, Ill.: IRI/SkyLight Training and Publishing, Inc.

Campbell, J. (1992, May). Laser disk portfolios: Total child assessment. *Educational Leadership,* p. 69–70.

Campbell, L. (1992). *Teaching and learning through multiple intelligences.* Seattle: New Horizons for Learning.

Chapman, C. (1993). *If the shoe fits…: How to develop multiple intelligences in the classroom.* Arlington Heights, Ill.: IRI/SkyLight Training and Publishing, Inc.

Combs, A. W. (1976). *What we know about learning and criteria for practice.* Adapted from a speech at the First National Conference on Grading Alternatives, Cleveland, OH. In Simon, S. B., & Bellanca, J. A., *Degrading the grading myths: A primer of alternatives to grades and marks,* (p. 6–9). Washington, D.C.: Association for Supervision and Curriculum Development.

Costa, A. L. (1991). *The school as a home for the mind: A collection of articles.* Arlington Heights, Ill.: IRI/SkyLight Training and Publishing, Inc.

Costa, A., Bellanca, J., & Fogarty, R. (1992b). *If minds matter: A foreword to the future (Vol. 2).* Arlington Heights, Ill.: IRI/SkyLight Training and Publishing, Inc.

Csikszentmihalyi, M. (1990). *Flow: The psychology of optimal experience.* New York: Harper & Row.

de Bono, E. (1992). *Serious creativity: Using the power for lateral thinking to create new ideas.* New York: Harper-Collins Publishers, Inc.

de Bono, E. (1985). *Six thinking hats.* Boston: Little, Brown.

de Bono, E. (1983). The direct teaching of thinking as a skill. *Phi Delta Kappan, 64*(1), 703–708.

Deming, W. E. (1986). *Out of the crisis.* Cambridge, MA: MIT Center for Advanced Engineering Study.

Dickinson, D. (1987). *New developments in cognitive research.* Seattle: New Horizons for Learning.

Diez, M. E., & Moon, C. J. (1992, May). What do we want students to know?…And other important questions. *Educational Leadership,* p. 38–41.

Eisner, E. W. (1993, February). Why standards may not improve schools. *Educational Leadership*, p. 22–23.

Feuerstein, R., Rand, Y., Hoffman, M., & Miller, R. (1980). *Instrumental enrichment: An intervention program for cognitive modifiability*. Baltimore: University Park Press.

Fogarty, R. (1994). *The mindful school: How to teach for metacognitive reflection*. Arlington Heights, Ill.: IRI/SkyLight Training and Publishing, Inc.

Fogarty, R. (Ed.). (1993). *The multiage classroom: A collection*. Arlington Heights, Ill.: IRI/SkyLight Training and Publishing, Inc.

Fogarty, R. (1992a). Teaching for transfer. In A. L. Costa, J. A. Bellanca, & R. Fogarty (Eds.), *If minds matter: A foreword to the future, Volume I* (p. 211–223). Arlington Heights, Ill.: IRI/SkyLight Training and Publishing, Inc.

Fogarty, R. (1992b). The most significant outcome. In A. L. Costa, J. A. Bellanca, and R. Fogarty (Eds.), *If minds matter: A foreword to the future, Volume II* (p. 349–353). Arlington Heights, Ill.: IRI/SkyLight Training and Publishing, Inc.

Fogarty, R. (1991). *The mindful school: How to integrate the curricula*. Arlington Heights, Ill.: IRI/SkyLight Training and Publishing, Inc.

Fogarty, R., & Bellanca, J. (1989). *Patterns for thinking: Patterns for transfer*. Arlington Heights, Ill.: IRI/SkyLight Training and Publishing, Inc.

Fogarty, R., Perkins, D., & Barell, J. (1992). *The mindful school: How to teach for transfer*. Arlington Heights, Ill.: IRI/SkyLight Training and Publishing, Inc.

Gardner, H. (1993). *Multiple Intelligences: The theory in practice*. New York: Basic Books.

Gardner, H. (1983). *Frames of mind*. New York: Basic Books.

Gardner, H., & Hatch, T. (1990). *Multiple intelligences go to school: Educational implications of the theory of multiple intelligences* (Report No. 4). New York: Center for Technology in Education.

Goodlad, J. I. (1984). *A place called school*. New York: McGraw-Hill.

Hamm, M., & Adams, D. (1991, May). Portfolio: It's not just for artists anymore. *The Science Teacher*, p. 18–21.

Hansen, J. (1992, May). Literacy portfolios: Helping students know themselves. *Educational Leadership*, p. 66–68.

Herman, J. L. (1992, May). What research tells us about good assessment. *Educational Leadership*, p. 74–78.

Hills, J. R. (1991, March). Apathy concerning grading and testing. *Phi Delta Kappan*, p. 540–545.

Jones, B. F., Palincsar, A. S., Ogle, D. S., & Carr, E. G. (Eds.). (1987). *Strategic teaching and learning: Cognitive instruction in the content areas.* Alexandria, VA: Association for Supervision and Curriculum Development.

Joyce, J. (1964). *A portrait of the artist as a young man.* New York: Viking Press.

Kallick, B. (1992). Evaluation: A collaborative process. In A. L. Costa, J. A. Bellanca, & R. Fogarty (Eds.), *If minds matter: A foreword to the future, Volume II* (p. 313–319). Arlington Heights, Ill.: IRI/SkyLight Training and Publishing, Inc.

Kirschenbaum, H., Simon, S., & Napier, R. (1971). *Wad-ja-get? The grading game in American education.* New York: Hart Publishing.

Knight, P. (1992, May). How I use portfolios in mathematics. *Educational Leadership*, p. 71–72.

Kohn, A. (1992). *No contest: The case against competition* (rev. ed.), Boston: Houghton Mifflin Company.

Kohn, A. (1991, March) Caring kids: The role of the schools. *Phi Delta Kappan*, p. 496–506.

Marzano, R. J., & Costa, A. L. (1988, May). Question: Do standardized tests measure general cognitive skills? Answer: No. *Educational Leadership*, p. 66–71.

McTighe, J., & Lyman, F. T. (1992). Mind tools for matters of the mind. In A. L. Costa, J. A. Bellanca, & R. Fogarty (Eds.), *If minds matter: A foreword to the future, Volume II* (p. 71–90). Arlington Heights, Ill.: IRI/SkyLight Training and Publishing, Inc.

North Central Regional Educational Laboratory (NCREL). (1991a). *Schools that work: The research advantage.* (Guidebook #4, Alternatives for Measuring Performance). Oak Brook, IL: Author.

North Central Regional Educational Laboratory (NCREL). (1991b). *Alternative assessment: Policy beliefs.* No. 15 & 16. Oak Brook, IL: Author.

Ogle, D. (1986). K-W-L: A teaching model that develops active reading of expository text. *The Reading Teacher, 6,* 564–570.

Palincsar, A. S., & Winn, J. (Eds.). (1990). Assessment models focused on new conceptions of achievement and reasoning. Symposium at the International Conference of the American Educational Research Association. [San Francisco, CA, March 27–31, 1989]. *International Journal of Educational Research, 10*(5), 409–483.

Perkins, D., & Salomon, G. (1992). The science and art of transfer. In A. L. Costa, J. A. Bellanca, & R. Fogarty (Eds.), *If minds matter: A foreword to the future, Volume I* (p. 201–209). Arlington Heights, Ill.: IRI/SkyLight Training and Publishing, Inc.

Shavelson, R. S., & Baxter, G. P. (1992, May). What we've learned about assessing hands-on science. *Educational Leadership*, p. 20–25.

Simon, S. B., & Bellanca, J. A. (Eds.). (1976). *Degrading the grading myths: A primer of alternatives to grades and marks.* Washington, D.C.: Association for Supervision and Curriculum Development.

Sizer, T. (1984). *Horace's compromise: The dilemma of the American high school.* Updated Ed. Boston: Houghton-Mifflin.

Sizer, T. R., & Rogers, B. (1993, February). Designing standards: Achieving the delicate balance. *Educational Leadership*, p. 67–72.

Sternberg, R. J. (1990). *Metaphors of mind: Conceptions of the nature of intelligence.* New York: Viking.

Stiggins, R. J. (1985, October). Improving assessment where it means the most: In the classroom. *Educational Leadership*, p. 69–74.

Tyler, R. W. (1949). *Basic principles of curriculum and instruction.* Chicago: University of Chicago Press.

U. S. Department of Labor. (1992, April). *Learning a living: A blueprint for high performance.* (A SCANS report for America 2000). Washington, D.C.: The Secretary's Commission on Achieving Necessary Skills.

Vickery, T. R. (1988, February). Learning from an outcomes-driven school district. *Educational Leadership*, p. 52–56.

Wiggins, G. (1992, May). Creating tests worth taking. *Educational Leadership*, p. 26–33.

Williams, R. B. (1993). *More than 50 ways to build team consensus.* Arlington Heights, Ill.: IRI/SkyLight Training and Publishing, Inc.

Winograd, P., & Gaskins, R. W. (1992). Metacogition: Matters of the mind, matters of the heart. In A. L. Costa, J. A. Bellanca, & R. Fogarty (Eds.), *If minds matter: A foreword to the future, Volume I* (p. 225–238). Arlington Heights, Ill.: IRI/SkyLight Training and Publishing, Inc.

Wolf, D. P. (1989, April). Portfolio assessment: Sampling student work. *Educational Leadership*, p. 35–39.

Wolf, D. P., LeMahieu, P. G., & Eresh, J. (1992, May). Good measure: Assessment as a tool for educational reform. *Educational Leadership*, p. 8–13.

World-Class Standards…For World-Class Kids. (1991). Kentucky Department of Education. Information on 1991–1992 Assessments.

Worthen, B. R. (1993, February). Critical issues that will determine the future of alternative assessment. *Phi Delta Kappan*, p. 444–456.

Index

Notes

There are **one-story** intellects, **two-story** intellects, and **three-story** intellects with skylights.

All fact collectors, who have no aim beyond their facts, are **one-story** minds.

Two-story minds compare, reason, generalize, using the labors of the fact collectors as well as their own.

Three-story minds idealize, imagine, predict—their best illumination comes from above, through the **skylight**.

—Oliver Wendell Holmes

PROFESSIONAL DEVELOPMENT

We Prepare Your Teachers Today
for the Classrooms of Tomorrow

Learn from Our Books and from Our Authors!

Ignite Learning in Your School or District.

SkyLight's team of classroom-experienced consultants can help you foster systemic change for increased student achievement.

Professional development is a process not an event. SkyLight's experienced practitioners drive the creation of our on-site professional development programs, graduate courses, research-based publications, interactive video courses, teacher-friendly training materials, and online resources—call SkyLight Professional Development today.

SkyLight specializes in three professional development areas.

Specialty #

Best Practices

We **model** the best practices that result in improved student performance and guided applications.

Specialty #

Making the Innovations Last

We help set up **support** systems that make innovations part of everyday practice in the long-term systemic improvement of your school or district.

Specialty #

How to Assess the Results

We prepare your school leaders to encourage and **assess** teacher growth, **measure** student achievement, and **evaluate** program success.

Contact the SkyLight team and begin a process toward long-term results.

2626 S. Clearbrook Dr., Arlington Heights, IL 60005
800-348-4474 • 847-290-6600 • FAX 847-290-6609
info@skylightedu.com • www.skylightedu.com